An Essay concerning Human Misunderstanding

Hank Youngman

2024

The following text is an informal essay. Parts have been fictionalized in varying degrees, for various purposes. The text is meant as literary entertainment only. The author bears no responsibility for any further inferences on the part of the reader. Citations and paraphrased text by other authors have been credited according to the MLA citation guidelines.

List of Contents

1. Overview

A Glance Ahead

In the preface to *The Sickness Unto Death*, Kierkegaard sets the standard for "the edifying" through the qualitative difference between "that sort of learning which is 'indifferent,'" and the kind of learning aware of "the reality of personal experience." The former kind he calls a "scientific aloofness from life," which he considers a self-serving indulgence, a dry affair made no nobler for its devotion to knowledge than it is wasted in having nothing to show for it. The latter, however, is not to be mistaken for empty pathos – an argument must be convincing, and its power of conviction must appeal to the healthy mind. Kierkegaard's meticulous approach to his treatise is proof of this. Therefore, though an inference void of humanity is a dud at best, an overt awareness of the human element is no excuse to deviate from reason; it is just that reason must neither stop short of humanity nor grasp beyond it. The edifying is about refined knowledge: not an excess or a limitation in scope, but a directedness of purpose. Having strongly agreed with the Danish philosopher, I have decided to begin my essay by letting the reader know that I have read Kierkegaard.

Further tuning into that strange brilliant book that is part theoretical science and part Christian poeticism, worded in language so academic I would have called it comprehensible were it any less, I have been so influenced by Kierkegaard's devotion to cognitive balance that I have not written anything without it in mind since – not even my fiction (nor poetry) have been spared the ambition. For the same reason, I have come to dislike both op-eds and scientific papers; it is for their deprivation of this balance that both fail in their purpose, as one fails to convince because of its hollowness, and the other does not even care to convince – only to state what may be true without daring call it so. A good text, I have concluded, ought to be scientific, in as far as it stands to reason, no less educated than sane, as its standard of inference, and it must maintain a moral tendency, in as far as it aims to be relevant to the lives of people, something which can in no instance, not even in the most boring examples, be ever considered truly dry – for any and all facts of human observance, life foremost, are governed by a moral reality, and abundant in such humanist lessons that the observer's interest or disinterest in them does little to alter the fact of their presence. The sensibility to notice them is a virtue; the pride in dismissing them is a misunderstanding – of what, you will discover as you read on.

Which raises an interesting point: in spite of their importance, many books like these, Kierkegaard's included, are difficult to come by in the average bookstore. This does not bode well for our intellectual inheritance. I do not consider it proof of deliberate censorship; it is easier to posit the law of demand than it is to prove a conscious swindle. However, the fact that popular demand has such a strong influence over culture, to the degree that authors appear to have been effectively banned from countries for the simple fact that they will not sell, is reason enough to suspect a kind of tyranny that is not to be underestimated for its randomness; spontaneity is not the antithesis of disaster. This is why I have dared to speculate in favor of self-importance: those of us who write must produce more books of this kind – the kind that a disastrous spontaneity ignores, and the kind that, if there ever is a sentient censor, will only engage his attention to ensure that there is nobody who cares to read them. Intellect is seldom in demand; but its guarantee is that of a persistent supply.

An Essay Concerning Human Misunderstanding is the central entry in a loosely related series of essays, themselves composed of even smaller essays, each building up the main argument of its respective release. It began as a side-trek to my fiction, and with the purpose of addressing what the former has not effectively revealed for its lack of directness. By a paradox that is at once cynical and optimistic, I blame it on my excess of subtlety (and not a bit of irony). And so, I have opted to code my message in a different format: not poetically mysterious, but poetically clear; not symbolic and interpretative, but symbolic and to the point; and not meant to entertain in part an impatient audience in-between the bits of philosophy, but meant entirely to entertain an intelligent audience, and specifically by those bits of philosophy I have otherwise tried to smuggle in with the action and suspense.

Just a while ago, I wrote *Pythagoras' Prison* as a prequel to what I write here; as a preemptive addressing of a common complaint I expect to hear in regards to some of the arguments I make. It is a criticism of the modern obsession with numbers as the substitute for meaning. It turned out more poetic than I expected, though (I hope) it is all the greater achievement for its reliance on symbol. I am not quite as indirect here; nor have I set out to address a complaint before the fact. Rather, I aim to present an argument. I mean to establish, before all, a few points about understanding and misunderstanding, about how we get to each state, and how we go about the sources that guide us. I do address the occasional contradiction when I am confident I can anticipate one, but I am more interested in answering honest questions than in predicting hostile objections.

Through my semantic and social and on occasion historical inferences, I try to trace a set of moral inferences, which I hold to be no more than the ethical implications of human cognition. Hence, Kierkegaard's likeness on the front cover. I do not intend to name names or to point fingers. I am not one to channel rage on anybody. Nor do I intend to clutter my paper with quotations for the sake of ornament. This is a caveat for footnote fetishists. I reference where I must, mostly to credit people, but, in general, I do not see the point in shoehorning text by other writers just to look smart. The novel thoughts I present here are by and large my own unless I specifically state otherwise. Anything in-between is either general knowledge or an obscure reference. Having said all that, my essay does have, in parts, an argumentative structure. So if you are indifferent regarding the abundance of citations, but do enjoy a logical construction or deconstruction, especially of modern-day passions, this essay has the kind of content you might like – from the meaning of words, as in the structuring of sense, to the meaning of liberty, intelligence, sanity, and the revelation they cumulatively make up. Seeing as we are only at the introduction of a much longer essay, the following should go without saying, except to confirm: there is a lot more than what I have listed in this paragraph.

And as I lead into the thematic introduction, as usual, I will wish you a good time reading; in addition to being scientific and edifying, I try to be entertaining. I only ask that you entertain my thoughts in return. I do not seek to win over anybody to my side. People are free to agree with me on one point and disagree on another. And yes, they may disagree with all of my points if they so desire. Ideally, readers will make the correct decisions independently of my attitude. Writing this, I feel like Moses striking the rock at one moment, and the Water Seller in the rain the next: offering something that I would be arrogant to claim is of me, offering something that I believe is essential to our survival, and offering something that I reckon people have at their full disposal anyway. But there is a redeeming clause to that sentiment: I am not opposed to the downpour; I have never dreamed that "the clouds went dry" (Steinman, "Water Seller"). I merely ask that, come what may, you stand up (*you fools!*) and if you do not buy my water, you at least harvest some of the rain. The opposite has you lounging in the mud (*you dogs!*) and both my water and the showers will have been for nothing.

<u>On Titles and Rationale</u>

By the method of linguistic compression, which methodology I have demonstrated not too long ago in exemplary theory (*Chapbooks Trilogy*, 75), I have summed up the foreword to this essay in its very title. I will now proceed to unpack it. Once the relationship between the five words has been studied in their communicative intent, the goal of my essay will have become apparent, unambiguous, and as easy to remember as the simple reference that contains it. I will explain more of the method itself in my next publication. For the time being, suffice it to say that this chapter presents the reversal of linguistic compression, and a constituent process of poetic analysis.

An Essay concerning Human Misunderstanding is not a phrase I have chosen on pure whim, or as a fleeting spoof of John Locke's epic. As far as it concerns the 17th century philosopher, it is to bring to attention the fact that, for all that has been said on the subject in the meantime, human understanding (understanding of human understanding not least), has improved very little since the Enlightenment. The illusion of progress has proven no more than an expensive sidegrade – proof of substitution rather than an accumulation of knowledge: we have gained some understanding in the natural sciences, but we have lost the same amount in the humanities; we appear to have understood digital processes, but only at the expense of our mental agency; and though we have come to understand a lot about the earth, we have mostly forgotten about its rational inhabitants. And so, seeing as the Age of Reason has acquired its bizarro-spinoff in the Age of Narrative, I have found myself contemplating if my literary ambition would be best repurposed, in the sense of the nobleness of the agenda, to the creation of an essay on the matters that concern us most. A variation of Locke's original, instead of focusing on innate and acquired knowledge, which would have been a matter of great concern to the empiricists, my paper would address inherited knowledge and acquired misknowledge, which seems to me is the burden that has come to weigh down on the current iteration of the common era. And so, I have set out to write a bit on what we have forgotten and what we have misunderstood, which, you will find, are really one and the same.

Though the aforementioned reference is deliberate, the connection between my essay and the title it emulates does not really go far beyond it. Of Locke, I know about as much as any man not passionate about Empiricism should. For what it's worth, I have picked up two of his essays and even bought them – they currently occupy a place on my shelf between *War and Peace* and *Bleak House*. I understand if the reader finds Locke a bit on the dull side as far as pretentious reading lists go, which is an unfortunate effect of age (whose age it is I leave ambiguous, for I cannot be certain of the answer myself), and for this reason I will try to avoid those traits about which datedness I agree. But enough about the overt part of the reference.

I use the back end of my title to call forth another piece, this one by a German author, which, though unwittingly made assigned reading in my high school, did little to make me depressed, but somehow went a long way in helping me see history as a pattern not of events or reactions to circumstance, but of flukes in reasoning, followed by series of rational recuperation, and sentenced to a wicked loop in its inevitable relapse. The author in question is Goethe, with whom I tend to disagree on other matters, and the book you might have guessed already – it is *The Sorrows of Young Werther*: an eighteenth century epistolary novella on the tragic extreme of oneitis. It contains a short expression of wisdom that was, as far as I could tell at the time, the only thing to get out of it. In the opening letter, the main character writes "Misunderstandings and neglect occasion more mischief in the world than even malice and wickedness. At all events, the latter two are of less frequent occurrence." *Oh Wilhelm!*

You may not agree with it on first glance, but with some consideration, you will find it impossible to reject; for even in instances of conscious malice, the decision to carry out one's malicious will is ultimately a lack of understanding of moral reality. Conversely, adherence to a moral code is indicative of an understanding that, though not necessarily intellectually integrated in the mind, is an apprehension of a reality to which the mind of the amoral person is as a ruptured eardrum is to music.

If you are willing to put this to the test, go ahead and ask somebody you know, *Why is charity a good thing?* If they willingly give to charity, though they may not be able to provide a coherent answer on the spot, the one thing their answer will contain will be traces of belief comparable to the belief in one's senses – a conviction formed not because of one's ability to prove it, but regardless of it. On the other hand, if their answer, though definite, reflects a learned catechism, such as an appeal to societal evolution or to self-serving empathy or even the odd religious recital, you will probably also find that they do not spend a lot of their income on charity – nor do they consider it particularly good. Press them a little further, and you might see the moral relativist begin to emerge. Of course, the scope of questions you may ask is not restrained to the question of charity. I chose it more or less at random. Here is another example. I have a friend who has on more than one occasion told me that there is nothing immoral in sleeping with a married woman – the flaw is with the woman for cheating, he argues, *if you don't do it, somebody else will; her husband's a cuckold either way,* so the trespasser is not to be blamed. I originally meant to ask him if he would rape a woman in war for the same reason – *even if you don't, the rest of your platoon will,* but I decided not to. For one, I knew he would answer in the negative. More importantly, I knew that he thought in the affirmative. He had not understood (nor does he understand to this day) that ethics prohibits profiting from evil, irrespective of the outcome – the only right response to evil is to reject it. There is much you can predict concerning a person's decisions, even in exceptional circumstances, if you know the extent to which they understand (or misunderstand) the arbiters of said choice. Morality is chief among them.

Evil, define it as you will, can only actualize in the absence of information, in the perversion of knowledge, or in missing perspective. Give it some thought, and you will see that it is true: from heredity to stupor to childhood trauma to power-induced insanity – no matter the particular cause, the practitioner of evil is ever a villain to understanding before he becomes a villain to anything else. He has either been denied some bit of knowledge, or he has chosen to reject it – all the same, he is lacking in apprehension. There is always something wrong, some cognitive hindrance or weakness of character that turns intellectual disintegration into immoral commitment. Why else do you think dictators must rely on indoctrination to get their people to comply with unlawful governance? And why would you say these same dictators despise philosophy? Perhaps, it is because they are just lucid enough to understand the threat that further understanding poses, even to their own crooked volition. An even better question could be: why do most self-assured people exhibit this same attitude towards deeper thought – and the best answer is to leave the implications of this *implicit*.

This fear of understanding, of a kind that results in either conscious or unconscious rejection of knowledge, might be considered by some a possible challenge to what I have been discussing so far, but in reality it only pushes the fact of misunderstanding one step back: instead of failure to see the fault in one's wrongdoing, one fails to apprehend the liberty in rising above it. Because even among the mentally sound, though the transgressor may know that something is true, yet he does not know the truth in it.[1] Think of a senior-year university textbook on advanced calculus. The majority of us understand that whatever has been printed on its pages is true, and yet, it is a truth that we do not know. It is the same with the moral dimension. The sane do not doubt it, but assuredness in it is not incompatible with ignorance of it. Why else do you suppose we see a philosophical world ridden with poorly defined concepts of good, of which none answer what good actually means? It is

---

[1] I got the idea for this reading MacDonald's commentary on damnation that went like so: "I dare not, cannot think that they refused the truth, knowing all that it was; but I think they refused the truth, knowing that it was true" ("It Shall Not be Forgiven"). Mine is not as sublime, but I hold it a reasonable take.

brimming with definitions because people sense it, and it is drowned in fallacies because people do not know it.

This should not deter us. It is ultimately a good sign that every culture worth its humanity has tried to codify the concept. It suggests an obligation to understand, and it is shared by all of mankind. Not only the concept of good, but everything about the world as we know it and as we learn about it. Responding to this obligation is our only means of keeping evil at bay – from outside and within. It is the fundamental proof of humanity. The more effective we are at explaining reality, and the more we practice communicating it, the less likely we are to fall victims to the subhuman rationale of the tyrant or the happy slave. Do not judge my use of the subhuman epithet by the way. If you can argue that, first, you are human, second, that you would be neither a tyrant nor a slave, and third, that your rationale for it is that no man should be either a tyrant or a slave, then the mentality that is either has been destined to an inhuman epithet; unless you have a reason to call it superhuman, the only modifier left is the one I have employed. In conclusion: practically, understanding keeps humanity safe; ontologically, it maintains it.

The Silent Indoctrinator

Before he got famous for crime, Mario Puzo wrote a book called *The Dark Arena*. It is rather prominently a story about misunderstanding – about general confusion, from neuroses to tragic flaws to total insanity, about people with limited knowledge doing things with limited ethics, about consequences much more dire than the imperfect but likeable protagonist could have ever predicted or deserved; stylistically, it is a precursor to what one might expect from Puzo given his literary reputation, with the exception that, instead of adding romance to crime, it takes the romance out of contemporary romance: set (mostly) in post-war Germany, a young American returns as a civilian to look for whatever place fate had destined for him outside the army. The plot follows a stream of events which underlying theme is disillusion: disillusion with the nobility of war, disillusion with the bureaucratic system some mistake for order, disillusion with people one would call friends (or at least friendly), disillusion with the sanctity of life, and, evident at both the beginning and the end, disillusion with the idea that there even is such a thing as a place in life.

The protagonist, one Walter Mosca, is disillusioned even with himself. The beginning of the story shows him returning to his family in the US, and finding himself a stranger in his homeland. In the conclusion, now in Germany, after having tried to become assimilated as a German citizen, Walter Mosca again finds himself a stranger, this time in his new homeland: the land where he had met a woman he loved, the land where he became a father, and the land he just about accepted as his own. Like Camus' character that is now a cliché to even reference, he is one without sense and without feeling and without a goal in life, but, unlike Camus' character, he did not get there by being a senseless, insensitive nihilist – on the contrary, he went in being a confused hedonist: a young untamed man with just enough heart to feel the injustice of the world he has inherited.

Character writing aside, however, I believe the most impressive literary achievement of this novel is Puzo's ability to present such a convincing image of the misery German citizens suffered following the Second World War, that, irrespective of one's contempt for the enemy, it is hard not to feel any sympathy for the people caught up in a misfortune they did not directly cause. This is not for the fact that the average citizen was mostly innocent, which is to most of us a well-known fact (and promptly ignored), nor for the fact that extreme poverty is a kind of torture we feel might be immanent and therefore easy to relate to (yet still promptly ignored), but because the closeness of the characters to the protagonist, their presence in the plot, their stories and the subplots they form, are all so intense and so capable of forming their own microcosm, that the reader (I am speaking from my subjective experience only) comes to know these people personally; no more fictions of historical fact (again, promptly ignored for their distance), they become real entities in the mind of the person experiencing them. To relate what I say here to the subject I have been discussing so far: the impersonal ignorance that prevents the reader from feeling the empathy he should is replaced with a personal knowledge that, like the conductor in an electric circuit, completes the trail between fact and understanding. No longer selectively stupid, the reader is no longer a selective sociopath.

And to follow up this bit of genius with a sprinkling of brilliance, Puzo does not shy away from the crimes against humanity committed by this nation for which the reader is supposed to feel a newfound empathy. Not only does he openly address the issue, but he addresses it with taste – it is not overdone, it does not try to moralize, and it does not try to inspire any sense of misery outside what the reader feels is the appropriate amount on his own accord. The most poignant instant of the theme is a conversation between a Jewish man and a German professor, of whom the former grew up in a concentration camp, and the latter's son is being tried at Nuremberg. The conversation is about this very subject.

The professor makes no attempt to deny his son's crimes. On the contrary, he even admits that, as his son has turned into a monster, which he likens to an illness, he must also perish because of it. His son apparently shares the sentiment (189). This illness, its symptoms and its cause, are not that dissimilar from the change in Mosca's personality. They both began as reasonably average youths, whose rearing should have resulted in virtue, but, coming out of the war, they emerge as alienated, selfish people; one bordering on sociopathic under the right circumstances, the other thoroughly sociopathic because of the circumstances. The professor goes through a psychological hell trying to make sense of it. He has not fought in the war, nor has he met many people visibly transformed by the experience, so he cannot connect the dots. Leo, his collocutor, not as vindictive as one might expect, does not think there is any reason the old man should suffer so. The answer that comes to his mind is amnesia: "There was no other way, but before his head dropped onto the wooden table he thought hazily of a wonderful solution, at every execution a drug be given to the loved ones, a drug of forgetfulness" (190)... He wonders if the professor could be made to forget his son, and it is regarding this hasty conclusion that I hold a contention, and over which I warn the reader not to take Puzo's suggestion, if it even is his suggestion, as a viable solution.

Because it is only by this suffering that the professor knows that he was wrong. He would not feel the same way had Germany won the war, or had he been kept oblivious of his son's crimes. He would have been proud of his military heroism, he might have remained content with his government, and he might have never felt sympathy for the people whose oppression was to him a matter of little (if any) concern. Leo observes as much himself; the professor was quite at peace during the height of the Third Reich. "This man, well educated, knowing right from wrong, who out of fear, cowardice, impotence... Slept warm in his bed, ate well, and earned it all with a helpless shrug, an easy resignation" (188). To make him forget the trauma that shook him out of his comfort would be to make him return to his comfort, to his easy resignation and the helpless shrug. He was selectively stupid for a time, and, therefore, he was selectively sociopathic. Now, he is painfully aware, and ignorance cannot be bliss. You may call it guilt, you may call it a rite of passage, you may call it a wage of sin – it is a tool of truth. Having done the crime morally, the only thing for this man is to be either a penitent opponent of the Nazi regime, or a content supporter of the Nazi regime. You either nod your head, or you bend the knee. There is no redemption without penance. Amnesia is not the cure. It is relapse.

But supposing that it is possible for a man to undergo a complete change of disposition, to become transformed from a criminal to a virtuous man (interpret the scope of this expression to whichever length you desire) by some process in the nervous system, a hormonal or electrical influence to mark the change, initiated by a painful event in the real world and now independent of it, such that, for the sake of argument, it is possible to preserve as a positive change sans the memory of the actual event, and in a way that the person in question will not be tempted, even without the tax of memory, to repeat a similar transgression, for the change is entirely physical and potent in its physicality alone, thus presently wholly separate from the memory in question, then I would argue that such therapy, were it performed on a patient, would be a worse disservice to him than to let him live knowing. This is because, in making him forget the event, you will have made him into an unreal person – you will have turned his personality into a script; something closer to Hamlet's personal history, i.e. a personhood imposed, as opposed a personhood developed with mediation of the subject himself. From the perspective of our patient, the event that made him what he is will never have happened. From his perspective, he is what he is without any reason for it whatsoever. He was not transformed; he was not even formed; he is just there, convinced of something and able to explain nothing. He cannot question it or change it, for it is thoroughly ingrained in him. He is not even allowed the dignity to call it his will. And though he may be content, you will have merely turned your patient from a troubled man into a happy program. Into a creature of an easy shrug and helpless resignation.

It would be a bizarre kind of indoctrination: an indoctrination void of language. It would be more effective than any propaganda one might conceive, though less intelligent than any attempt at brainwashing prior to it. To do away with the mind and let the chemistry in one's body be the sole arbiter of his character. It would be as if, having read *The Dark Arena* and so come to commiserate with the post-war German citizen, I could forget that I have learned about the suffering these citizens endured, yet maintain the feeling of sympathy I had developed for them – but now, instead of a sympathy built on experiencing the suffering of innocents, it will be a sympathy for people I recognize not as innocent, but as thoroughly guilty. Without the memory, my just condemnation will have turned into an unjustified forgiveness, and my righteous convictions will have become a confused whim.

And while the kind of medicine that could do that is (as far as I know) only speculative, the technique itself is, I have found, very much real. Do note that the professor's son is very similar, in having become a monster, to Mosca himself, and even more so, to Mosca's friends: they have all either committed or witnessed crime during the war and after it; Wolf is a sadistic intelligence officer not hesitating to torture people, and Eddie Cassin sexually abuses a vulnerable woman. The only difference is that, being on the winning team, they have not been forced onto the penitent team. They were given the glory of victory and the privilege of triumph, and so, feeling as good as they do, they cannot see their own transformations for what they are. The reason for it all is this selective amnesia, brought about by the feel-good conclusion of the tragedy, safeguarding the exalted state against the check of reason.

The danger in this is that it is not a phenomenon restricted to fiction. While we do not have the pill, in the real world, it is exactly what I said: indoctrination without language. It is letting a person feel what he will, and making sure he does not think what he will not. Take away a person's sensibility for language, and you are halfway there. Make him feel things he is unable to express (the more potent the more effective; the more complex the less penetrable), and you will have accomplished your mission. Replace culture with whatever influences both steps, and you will find that the rest develops on its own. There will be people who are transformed at every instant, whose personalities keep changing to the whim of the times (or to the will of whoever is pulling their strings), and able to make nothing of it. A complete rebirth, a mute indoctrinator, and silent chaos. Brother against brother, one automaton clinking, another clanking, and neither knowing.

Perhaps the predictive (or the historically speculative) part of my belief relies too much on hope to count as fact. Perhaps I am being too optimistic. In that case, so be it. Hope gets too much bad rep anyway. Some of it is deserved, but the kind I exhibit here is not the wishful kind about winning the lottery or leading a happy family life (which I have found is about as likely as winning the lottery), but that men and women are inherently good.

This is not to say that the majority of our kind are good in practice. Only that whatever problems there exist are mostly a result of confusion: sometimes volitional, and often too thorough to buckle to explanation, but always a loss of clarity preceding the gain in wickedness. And so, I do not suppose it is the kind of hope by which my drive should be sentenced to forfeit its claim to objectivity. I do not merely hope passively. I try to address the problem. As such, you will find my belief closer to a motive, as opposed to fancy. When a fisherman steers his boat to where he hopes he will find marlin, you do not call him whimsical for his conviction; you call him reasonable for following it.

Now, take note that my endorsement of Goethe's proposition should not be read as an attempt to downplay evil. *Evil is not evil, guys, it's just stupid!* On the contrary, I aim to draw attention to the danger of misunderstanding: the less we know, the more liable we are to fall victims to the side-effects of ignorance. Misunderstanding will not only make us the victims of evil rulers, imagine them as you wish, but it will also turn us evil in the process. No sooner will a man mistake his brother for his enemy than he will mistreat him, and there is no fiercer enemy to freedom than a tyrant who can sow hatred between brothers.

A Literal Swindle

The Enemy's Method in Theory

Nor would that present any serious challenge to the tyrant – all he would need to do would be to change the definition of brotherhood: to obscure it to some extent, just enough to cause a lack of understanding, and to simply wait until misunderstanding turns to malice. Being the king of deception (his own before the rest), he will make sure that it does.

It is a risk to propose a blatant lie early in the interaction. It is also a risk to make a claim that can be made the subject of debate. To maximize its chance of acceptance, a lie must be presented in a format immune to effective reaction, i.e. to all negative reaction save the safe kind that serves as its immunization. To begin, a lie must be smuggled through an idea so visibly distant from the deception it carries, that the only people to notice it will be the paranoid – analogous to an overreaction of the immune system, they are a group whose revolt can be written off to mental instability more so than reasonable skepticism. Keep in mind, it is reason that kills a lie – tactless disagreement merely adds to the confusion. Suppose I want to convince you that your brother is your enemy. I could try to tell you, right away, that he is not in fact your brother, but, if I did, you would call out my lie on the spot. I must be more tactical if I am to succeed. Therefore, I will merely suggest that the antonym of *abstract* is *real*: the way that a rock, being concrete, is real, but that artistic value, being abstract, is not. I have actually heard this at a university lecture. If you can begin to see a pattern between my philosophy and sowing discord between you and your brother, I will inform you that tracing patterns when there are none is a symptom of mental illness. On this, you must agree, for it is backed by the authority of science; your only options, should you choose to proceed with your accusation, will be insanity and ignorance. Now observe what I have done: though I have awoken some semblance of a reasonable reaction, it was a reasonably weak resistance, and a short-lived one at that. And so, my lie has been immunized: when the time comes and it is exposed, it will be much more resistant to criticism, having once proven its reasonableness in the face of senseless opposition.

You may have also noticed that the process is symmetrical, for as the lie has been made immune to criticism, so has the potential critic been inoculated against criticizing. He has already accepted one fallacy; the next one is simply part of the course. The difference this time is that instead of a half-truth, you will be fed an error, which, harder to swallow on its own, should be edible now that you trust the chef. Do you agree that indirect language (think metaphor and its relatives), dealing with the abstract, is not factually real? After all, if we say of a poor man that he is rich, what we really mean is that he is happy – factually rich he is not. Nor was Napoleon ever the greatest man in the world (not even in cowboy boots), but a mere historically poignant person. It is worth noting: there has never been a halfwitted girl that held a conversation with a wolf, although, an extroverted personality can carry you far. Metaphor, sometimes accurate and sometimes total BS, is never something to be taken without a generous serving of salt.

Now, some of you might disagree with me on the matter to an extent, but I assure you that you have most likely fallen for the lie already, though you think you disagree with its premise. Next time you go outside, look upon any man that walks by you and ask yourself if he is your brother. If you answer in the positive, do accept my congratulations: you have defied the odds, and you have not been deceived. But if you answered in the negative, I will ask you to reconsider if you may have, after all, swallowed the narrative to which you have considered yourself immune throughout these paragraphs. You may have read what I said about *abstract* meaning *unreal* and disagreed: *numbers are abstract and yet they are real*, you may think to yourself, and you may even think *Metaphor doesn't need to be literal in order to be true!* and though you would be right, in varying degrees, the fact of the matter is that you still hold to the idea that the man you see on the street is not your brother.

But he is clearly not my brother, you might protest, *I don't even know him – and we clearly don't share the same parents!* And yet, is what we call siblinghood not merely the representative of a degree (as opposed to a necessity) of brotherhood? For mutual parents, and, ideally, a period of growing up together, is only an extent to which you can share the same experiences with another person – an extremely unique set of experiences, but only in kind, not in totality. Genes do not make up all there is to brotherhood. You have likely heard of people who served in the army being described as *brothers in arms*, of law-abiding Christians calling their flockmates *brother*, and outlaw bikers referring to their pack by the same designation. If you are a person of estimable cultural affinities, you also likely know a Texan singer who called his New Yorker friend a brother whom he loves – mind you, with an emotion much stronger than you would feel for an estranged biological brother.

Brotherhood, in its true sense, is a bond between men arising out of shared experience. The more intense the experience, the stronger the bond, and wherever one may imagine the potential for such an experience, there also one recognizes the spark of brotherhood. One's siblings are just a subset, and a conspicuous set of representatives. Consider just how much experience you share with your fellow man by the mere virtue of being man – and how much more you share with your compatriots, many of whom you have never met, yet you all speak the same language, have been affected by the same events in history, have come to visit similar places, and to understand places and events and feelings through the windows of the same cultural fortress; until the recent deception had taken root, how you might have shared the same joys and fears and aspirations, the same songs and customs and how you will have made similar plans in the common land you call your home. And farther still, beyond the concept of nationalism, how you could share those same things with a total stranger across the ocean. How is all of that subsidiary to genetics? Do these people not qualify as your brothers?

Well, sure, you might say, *But that's just metaphor!* And there you have it.

Metaphor and Language

Metaphor, as observed from the outside, has the appearance of a multi-layered contradiction. It is somewhere between an anomaly and an oddity. It just about does not belong in language as we understand it. You may call a man lionhearted, and no cardiologist will call you out on it. You may call a woman a cow, and the only zoologists to correct you would be the politically correct kind. You can call life hell, and theologians will likely agree. Metaphor sounds simple in daily use, but it is anything but if you consider its mechanism: you say one thing, you mean another, and, somehow, you are not a liar – not to yourself and not to anybody else. If your metaphor is understood, what has really transpired has been people hearing what you didn't mean and somehow understanding what you did mean. Weirdest of all is that this will have been precisely your intention.

Linguists have tried to answer this, mostly successfully, and, as part of their explanation, they tend to see metaphor as an iteration of language recognizable in two forms: a linguistic metaphor (in use) and a conceptual metaphor (in the mind). Linguistic metaphors are the expressions we all commonly recognize as metaphors – in the sentence, *that Neanderthal next-door is drilling at 6* AM *again,* the linguistic metaphor is exactly the expression you assume is the metaphor. Conceptual metaphors, on the other hand, are the structural connections that account for the understanding of linguistic metaphors. In the former example, the conceptual metaphor would be UNCIVILIZED PERSONS ARE NEANDERTHALS, or something to that extent. So, when somebody uses a linguistic metaphor, what they really use is a shortcut to its conceptual counterpart. You do not think of the phrases used, but of the cognitive connections with which they resonate.

With time, linguistic metaphors can get so conventionalized that a lexeme may acquire one of its metaphorical senses as its literal meaning. If you said that your boss was *an imbecile*, this would not refer to a mental disability with which he has been born, but rather, it would simply mean that you consider him an idiot. I used that example deliberately, as *idiot* was also an initially non-metaphoric expression with the rough meaning of *special*. When this happens, the conceptual metaphor moves from an underlying structure of indirect meaning to the dictionary definition, becoming the intended sense in the direct meaning of the word. The dynamic process of conceptualization becomes assimilated into a fixed frame.

The most prominent reason for this is the frequency of use of each form: a word that is used a lot with its metaphorical meaning but only rarely sees application in its original sense will likely undergo the conceptual shift, whereby its original sense becomes obsolete, and the indirect meaning becomes the conventional form. It is important to keep the following two facts in mind: convention dictates change (even on the conceptual level), and loss is as frequent a change as any other – even a loss of concept.

Though it may sound like a triumph of the indirect expression, this trend is actually detrimental to the metaphor: the conventionalized form can carry on without the conceptual process, in which event the conceptual structure is cast out. The once indirect sense remains, now considered direct, but the senses that have led to it are forgotten. It is why they are also called dead metaphors (Bowdle & Gentner 118). This is also how a metaphorical expression can turn into an idiom. Idioms are expressions which meanings we know not because we can predict them, as we do with metaphor, but because we have learned them. We have no other way of knowing what it really means to freeze the balls off a brass monkey or to have an uncle named Bob. You might be able to guess the speaker's meaning from the context, but you would not know why your uncle's name should not be Roger, or if something can, in the opposite scenario, boil the balls off a lead capuchin. Predictability is not a requirement in idiomatic expressions (Kovecsec, 254). The concept of predictability, in this sense, denotes whether an expression can signal, by itself, its own conceptual background. *Balls to the wall* has no such chance. A *fiery temper* just might. Hanks adds that the difference can be seen as a historical resonance in idiom as opposed to the conceptual predictability in active metaphor (26-27). And so, as long as we have access to the same semantic code by which we have inherited the expressions we learn, we can make sense of their indirect meanings without having to rely on rote recital. But it is a law of nature, no doubt, an addendum to the law of decay with an exclusively human spin, that there are bits of the semantic code to which our access has been severed, and of which we can therefore make no sense but the sense we have learned as the given, conventional form with delimited meaning. It is according to the same law that they must grow in number.

And there lies the rub: the loss of semantic knowledge will only increase, and there is no way of knowing to what degree sense has been lost but by its constant semantic testing, which one rarely (if ever) does. It could be that the majority of the expressions we have learned are just such conceptual skeletons, conventionalized for us to learn, word-for-word, as convention mandates, but which foundations are to us alien. You can probably see where this argument is going. What we see as the literal, definitive, solely valid and often original sense of an expression, may well be just a zombie-meaning shambling across the cityscapes of abandoned knowledge.

Metaphor and Brotherhood

As far as we can tell, the earliest mentions of the phrase *brother* refer to brotherhood by blood, or the literal meaning of a male sibling. And as far as we can tell, the metaphorical concept of brotherhood has been around since written text has been able to attest for it. English *brother*, etymologically close to Latin *frater*, with the meaning of biological brother, has a cognate in the Greek *phrater* and *phrator* meaning "member of a brotherhood, a clansman" and eventually as *phratria*, which refers to a clan or a political brotherhood (Partridge, 1183-84). While I am aware of the plausibility that the origin of the expression could have been the literal meaning, I do not think it is possible to argue with complete certainty that the metaphor lagged significantly behind, though, to make my point clear: I do not think that is at all relevant. It is not so important to argue which came first as much as it is to note the fact that the two uses appear early. There are no known instances of either being treated as a marked variant in its development.

This implies simultaneity, as neither use appears to conceptually precede the other. Factors that could be said to have influenced the order of their appearance across languages are rooted in circumstances outside of concept, belonging to that dimension of anthropology that theorizes well in as far as it speculates just as well, which, though likely to dictate the conceptual patterns to which societies and persons become attuned, being an extra-linguistic factor, are not the conceptual patterns they influence, irrespective of the connection between the one and the other. There is no reason to disregard the closeness in the appearance of the two uses, and conclude that whichever is of the biological domain came first, or even that whichever came first must be the *true* use, i.e. the only valid form of the expression. The certainty that they both appeared close enough in the timeline makes the fact of any historical interval where one existed without the other, if there ever was one, obsolete. The important piece of information is their proximity, and the important observation to make is their shared meaning. All this goes to bolster the case for a common motivator.[2]

I say this because the conceptual, analytic understanding is the best explanation for how the metaphor must have come about. It really has no consistently reliable competition. For one, we cannot call it the result of poeticism, as is common in metaphor, since there are no codes of brotherly conduct that we know of, or legends that utilize the motif of brotherhood as a romanticized ideal preceding the metaphor, as is the case with knighthood or soldiery. On the contrary, what the mythical record shows is biological brotherhood in its earthly reality: Cain and Abel, Romulus and Remus, Esau and Jacob, and the divine bickering of the Hellenistic pantheon to name a few general examples. The metaphor of brotherhood denoting a sacred connection between a man and another person cannot have come about from any idealized brotherhood one sees in legend, seeing as legend speaks mostly of rivalry and violence, and hardly of loyalty and self-sacrifice. Possible ideological influences are also unlikely. Though 20th century collectivism has been popularized as the movement that made camaraderie hip, the concept of brotherhood does not have an equivalent in ideological movements. Indeed, the term has been used in politics and religion, but this has been only second-degree utilization, after the metaphor had already become common, and in contexts evoking a system already formed, not one in its creation. I do not think Christians would have called themselves *brother* unless they believed they shared the same Father, nor will have revolutionaries in France fought for brotherhood unless the metaphor had already existed – surely, they were not looking for the kind of *fraternité* they observed among the nobility. For the same reason, an empirical explanation cannot cover the motivation for the idealized

---

[2] Motivation in the study of metaphor denotes the conceptual force influencing the conceptual structure.

metaphor either, seeing as what can be observed among siblings is hardly the kind of relationship that at all suggests a romantic conceptualization – rather, whatever concept may arise out of empirical observation is more likely to resonate with legends depicting sibling rivalry, as opposed to the kind of love suggested in the idealized sense. So I would warn against suggesting that, whoever came up with the term, saw the reality of brotherly hatred, not unlike the hostility between the wolf and its prey, somehow got the idea of brotherly love, seeing as he did not get an idea of wolfish love either, and went on to build upon it a metaphor that speaks of love and devotion and loyalty and all the expected virtue encompassed in the concept of brotherhood. At least, I do not believe it would catch on even if somebody did. Therefore, I suggest that the underlying idea was profound in its conception.

The best explanation for the indirect understanding of brotherhood is the conceptual metaphor BROTHERHOOD IS SHARED EXPERIENCE or BROTHERHOOD IS SHARED EXISTENCE. Not only is that the structural metaphor in the linguistic uses we can observe, but it is also the only link between the direct sense and its indirect counterpart. It is the only sense from which a bonding moral implication may arise.

Without the general conceptual structure, the specific understanding of siblinghood would be meaningless. One cannot first argue that brotherhood is not in fact about shared experience or a shared existence, but then argue that it is about shared parents. It would be like arguing that a bicycle is not something with wheels, but something with two wheels. To this, one might object that brotherhood is exclusively the kind of relation between a man and another person that exclusively covers shared parents, but that would conflict with such expressions as *your friend is more of a brother to you than your real brother*, or *your brother is not treating you very brotherly*. Clearly, those two expressions have personal, moral, and expectational senses, and become absurd if analyzed as if their core meaning is not the concept of a general shared experience (or existence), but shared parents. Consider the following expressions:[3]

> [1] Justin's been more of a brother than you've ever been.
> [2] That's not very brotherly of you.
> [3] Please do not call me bro. I am not your bro!
> [4] Francis saw the Gospel pattern of life calling him to be with his sisters and brothers in Christ.
> [5] he welcomed... onstage, calling him a "brother from another mother..."
> [6] We've been together 22 years. Gene is like a brother to me.
> [7] This conversation revives us the memory of a friend that was more than a brother to me.

Without the general scope of the conceptual metaphor, they lose their sense. If we assume that the concept of brotherhood is valid exclusively as a relationship between a man and another person with whom he shares the same biological parents, then the conceptual mirror of the examples above would produce absurdities such as [1L] *Justin has more of the same parents with me than you do*, or [2L] *You do not treat them as if you share the same parents* and "so on and so on" (Žižek). By analogy, the argument that brotherhood is conceptualized as siblinghood would be like saying that a bird is conceptualized as a creature with a beak, and therefore the conceptual metaphor FREEDOM IS A BIRD is built upon the idea that freedom has a beak. Therefore, by this same analogy, we need to look for the conceptual motivator in whichever realm best represents brotherhood's analogous wings. And, you will see, this common sense is in the realm of metaphor, not the conventionalized referent for siblinghood.

---

[3] The following are American English samples taken from magazines, TV, web, and news sources, found on *English-Corpora.org*. I use them here only to demonstrate that the expressions do exist in the English language, i.e. that I am not making them up; I have no interest in their frequency of use or other statistical data.

Examples [1] to [5] have a conceptually identifying function, whereas examples [6] and [7] are conceptually contrastive or comparative. Whereas the first five refer to somebody as a brother, by which they identify the person in question as a representative of brotherhood, the other two reference the conversational subject as somebody who is clearly not the speaker's brother, but is in some way close to the concept. This points us to a commonly cited difference between metaphor and simile, with simile being "always literally true because any two things must always be alike one way or another... in an indeterminate number of ways" (Glucksberg 68), meaning that, although metaphor and simile are alike, and they can be used, in a lot of instances, interchangeably without loss of meaning, simile as an expression is distinct in its awareness that the two domains are not the same.[4] This is important to note because it means that examples like [6] and [7] do in fact utilize the conventionalized, direct sense of the lexeme; [7] is perfectly sensible if reworded as [7L] *...the memory of a friend that was more (to me) than somebody with whom I might share the same parents.* Simile is the safety guard against misinterpretation. In directly calling for a comparison, it does not make bizarre identity-clauses. But to stop there is to give up the trail. The important question to ask regarding the simile examples is – *in what way?*[5]

---

[4] To clarify, as some people might see [1] as identical to [7], the use in [1] suggests that Justin is the speaker's brother, differing in degree as opposed to kind, as in he is *more a brother* than the collocutor, whereas [7] posits the friend as somebody who is not one's brother, but is superior to a brother in the comparison. Similarly, [3] is a statement about whether somebody is the speaker's "bro," not whether somebody is like a "bro" to the speaker. This is why we treat [1] and [3] as examples of metaphor, and [7] as simile.

[5] This is why a similarly reworded [6L] does not work out of context: it suggests a moral or a sentimental implication that is not self-evident, i.e. it must rely on an established standard or foreknowledge of the family unit to make the connection. It relies on a contextual hypernym, explained in another chapter (79).

In what way is a friend more than a brother? In what way is this person like a brother to you? It is simile, it calls for comparison, and so, it must validate the standard for comparison – one cannot liken the one to the other without some perceived similarity to justify it. You would not replace [6] with [6A] *He is like a Guinea pig to me* and argue that the meaning of the expression has remained unchanged; there must be a common sense between domains to connect the phrases in the intended sense in the context. The answer becomes clear when we look at examples [1] to [5]. It is the identifying uses that answer the standard for comparison. *In what way is a friend more than a brother? A friend is more than a brother in that he is more of a brother.*

I am not being mysterious to compensate for my looks. That really is what it says. And it is not all that confusing. The metaphor merely suggests that a friend is more than a biological brother in that a good friend is like an *actual* brother. In the same way that a bad king is not kingly because he is not like an actual king. Consider [7A] *Somebody with whom one shares experience is more than somebody with whom one shares the same parents,* and you will see it.[6] This also enables [6A] *He is like somebody with whom I share my existence,* which, though weirdly worded, nevertheless suggests the correct set of senses. Brotherhood, as a conceptual event, posits idealized moral and sentimental expectations superimposed on the conventionalized representative observable in mundane, terrestrial contexts. And the source of these expectations, as we saw earlier in this chapter, is an abstract concept, not a common phenomenon in the material world.

As far as I have been able to tell, examples [1] through [7] denote closeness, trust, and assumed familiarity. The negative example in [3] is especially expressive of that – *Do not speak to me as if we are close, for we are not.* Do note that it is not something you would tell a friend. [5] suggests solidarity, and [4] goes as far as shared Creation. I would sum up all of these senses in the

---

[6] Alternatively, [7A1] *A brother is more than a sibling.*

contextual hypernym of *shared existence* or, by extension, *shared experience*. I say that because closeness, trust, and assumed familiarity can only exist in a scene where the parties involved agree to share. Otherwise, it will not be a shared existence, but a contended existence; in which case closeness, trust, and assumed familiarity will be as they are today – hidden, boarded up, and hoping to evade the hordes of zombie-meanings flooding the streets of our once-great cities.

Brothers at Arms

Clearly, the concept of brotherhood is not about siblinghood, but a universal admittance of humanity. The only way to try and refute this would be to posit two categories: brotherhood₁ with the meaning of siblinghood, and brotherhood₂ with all of the other meanings, including the adjectival and the adverbial variations of the noun, with the stipulation that this second iteration must be inferior to the first in spite of its productivity. Then again, this would fail to address the motivation of the metaphor, and it would do nothing to actually discredit the conceptual foundation beyond wishing it away. Still, I would be open to accept it on account of the present state of affairs. It would only prove the point I made earlier: we are left with a delimited sense bereft of all the other senses, learned as a fixed phrase we utter not because we understand it, but because we have memorized it. And so considering the conceptual origin of the metaphor, when you say that, *Yes, we are all brothers – but that is only a metaphor!* what you are really saying is *Yes, we are all brothers – but that is only if we care about what that word means!*

Given the present condition, the only person one can regard as a brother is a person that one may not even consider a brother, for his behavior has not been necessarily brotherly; all this for a word no more sensible than the adjective which standard it fails to meet, now rendered meaningless without its conceptual structure, by which brotherly behavior has become the behavior of a sibling, hardly capable of setting any moral expectations on its own;

brotherly love is no more brotherly than it is love. This absurdity will be proclaimed reasonable, and reason will be proclaimed absurd; all because you were told that not just anyone can be your brother – no, not just anyone, but just anyone who happens to have been born of the same parents; he alone can be your brother, unlike all the other people, who, you were told, cannot be what your brother is not either.

With that, conflict between brothers can carry on uninterrupted, without the slightest notion of the underlying tragedy or any obligation to put an end to it. It is just as our tyrant intended. And do note that, in practice, biological brotherhood will come to mean nothing in the end. If the only thing that matters for the definition of brotherhood is shared heritage, then *nothing* else matters in brotherhood beyond getting the bigger share. I have a duty to persons, not blood – genetic or otherwise, no bond but the personal can interfere with my property. If I love you, I will honor you; I will see you as an equal. If I do not, you could be my clone for all I care. Devoid of brotherhood, proximity is a hazard, not a cause for celebration. I would prefer to keep my siblings at a distance, and I am sure their preferences would not differ from mine. And do we not see this happening, in history among the rich, and in the present dystopia just about everywhere?

Without the conceptual matrix, the expression is meaningless, save in that sole lexical instance that keeps it from becoming total nonsense. The word has been utterly impoverished, and brotherhood, though once meant to denote a close alliance, has in practice come to mean the opposite. Just as it has been the case with kingship and leadership and heroism, sacrifice of the self becomes a sacrifice for the self, with modern kings being egomaniacs, leadership being a career, and heroism the securing of status. It seems absurd, but absurdity, in the sense of a senseless kind of stupidity, is the logical outcome of neglecting indirect language, which, you will see in the third part, is precisely where sense is contained. It is why corruption in the abstract results in ruin of the concrete.

<u>Confusion in Kind: the Stone and the Statue</u>

Let us steer from profundity for a moment and consider two examples regarding the closing sentence of the previous chapter. Just as I did in *Pythagoras' Prison*, I will illustrate a piece of the problem by a review of trend. Being a mindless process, it is a breeding ground for mindless mishaps, and the place where concept first begins to shamble. I will talk about the trends of virtuous greed and promiscuous masculinity – the double standard of boisterous men, and the obsession of public intellectuals with the kind of paper on which nothing more intelligent than germs has ever resided. So, taking a break from profound brotherhood, let us briefly have some fun with profound silliness.

The obsession with wealth can by no means be said to have only recently surfaced in the world, but it is not a fetish marking an ancient continuity either. Instead, it is a love that becomes renewed with each generation, not stagnating as a classic, left to the mercy of the times, as do all remnants of the past, but regenerating itself with each rite of passage into materialist culture, as it is with all things bearing the illusion of timelessness. Every generation discovers it anew, and from a different perspective: the belief that money is power, that power really matters, and that to matter is the one virtue that matters truly. I have heard, (yes, often among simpletons, but most prominently among intellectuals), such expressions as *There is nothing wrong in wanting money*. On the one hand, it is true that there is nothing wrong in a man wanting money. In a society where money matters to live, to want to have money is to want to live. In a hypothetical society where money does not matter for survival, to want money would be no less moral than to want a stamp collection. There would be nothing wrong with that either. The conceptual perversion of the expression results from the attempt to use it as justification for desiring an excess of money. Consider how, in being a means for survival, an excess of money could only be an excess of survival, and how conceptually incoherent that is. Survival can only be measured up to a neutral, optimal point: a man who eats three times a day can be said to survive *more* than a man who eats three times a week, but he does not survive less than the man who eats ten times a day. Likewise, an excess of money does not satiate the natural urge to live. Just as greed is not the human urge to prosper. [7] Rather, it is the concept of *mirage* hijacking the concept of *insecurity*, and building up to a ridiculous confusion: there is nothing bad in being bad if being bad brings more good than it is good.

The promiscuous alpha male mentality is similarly related to a misunderstanding of excess, except that the error in its conceptual process is not the dismissal of vice, but the failure to understand the error with which it is being justified. There are men (maybe even the majority of men) who would judge a woman for sleeping around, but praise a man for doing the same. These are also men who do not hold this to be a double standard, because men and women, they argue, were built differently: having more testosterone, men have a stronger urge to mate, whereas women have less of both; therefore, it is tolerable for a man to sleep around because his urge is just so much greater than a woman's. Now, in regards the strength of the urge, I am not convinced; but even if we assume it is accurate, do we not unjustly limit the excuse by not applying it to similar behaviors? Violence, for instance, should be proclaimed tolerable among men, since testosterone also accounts for a tendency to hit things. *Ah, but that's a mistaken category!* a midwitted reader might protest, *Promiscuity is consensual whereas violence is not!* But what happens, in that case, to the relatively less intense urges of women? If promiscuity is not comparable to violence because there is consent on the part of the woman, does the fact of consent not suggest that the willing woman's urges are equally as strong as the man's? It would not be a consensual affair if the

---

[7] Do not mistake it for an argument for financial independence by the way; people who parrot the phrase dot not use it to justify honest labor.

woman agreed to intercourse without the same degree of desire –
it would be a case of coercion, at its most innocent manipulation,
not consent. So the man's behavior would certainly be
comparable to the dynamic of violence if we assume a
comparatively unwilling other. And, of course, if the urges of
both are equal, then the argument that testosterone absolves
men but condemns women fails at its conception. Justifying
sexual immorality in men either justifies sexual immorality in
women as well by the fact of consent, or it frames the process as
one of men pushing women into the very behavior men despise.
The adage that *A lock that is opened by many keys is a poor lock, but a
key that opens many locks is called a master key* makes for a poor
argument. A master key does not open just any lock – it only
opens locks designed specifically to be opened by it. So if a lock
that turns easily is a whore, then the master key that opens it is
but a whoremaster. Anyone who has at some point been (to
varying extent) deceived by this philosophy, has probably
recognized (in time) that the only women susceptible to the high
quality alpha male who mates a lot are women that this same
philosophy would brand low quality women on account of
allowing the self-proclaimed alpha male to mate as much as he
does. The status for being a real man is in the hands of
unqualified judges. So the conceptual error here, depending on
your tastes, can be absurd, ridiculous, or sad; men who hold to
this confusion the strongest are men who know very little of
keys, locks, and women. They do not understand themselves
either, seeing as they have a poor understanding of their own sex.
It is a blunder engendered by a misunderstanding of an abstract
instantiation: a mistake in regards the word chastity (the concept
of sexual morality) as exclusive to only one gender, specifically,
the gender so foreign to the confused speaker, that, to him, it does
not stand a chance to be understood as a partaker in a unisex
system of ethics.

So there you have two cases of confusion: concepts not
explored in their totality, but left to roam as shambling zombies,

taking their victims wherever they go. It is not nearly as epic as that of brotherhood, and not quite as conspiratorial (though I do not argue for a literal conspiracy in the desolation of brotherhood either). They are, all the same, equally as real, and it is important to guard against the ridiculous many as it is to guard against the serious few.

Abstract concepts are like a statue of a great person in history. Material objects are as stone. Now, a stone shaped to resemble a great person in history, though it will remain stone in matter, in substance, it will have become a monument. But it will never be the great person it represents. When a historical figure, now in no discernable shape whatsoever, comes to be represented by stone, the historical reality of the person in question is in no way impeded by the form. Though the person has never been a statue, the latter can stand for the person. Nor is the skeleton that used to be him that person, as no great person in history has ever been a pile of rotting bones. The deeds of man, his fame, and the narratives surrounding it are not defined by material means. They consist of abstract terms, not subjected to material reality, but approachable only by means conveying an intangible reality – identity, memory, historicity, method, impact, recognition...
Language validates what may be perceived by drawing both worlds (material and immaterial) into a universe of understanding, which itself cannot be but immaterial, although, as communication is not yet telepathic, cannot be conveyed but by material means. Which is why we must always keep in mind the interaction between the two. The moment you have written off the abstract in favor of what is commonly understood by the concrete, you will be left not with a stone that is now a monument to Caesar, nor to Caesar as represented by a statue, but with a weirdly shaped chunk of solid matter, and no legacy for anyone or anything, including the language we forget whenever we lose touch with the words we utter. Reality is rendered to rotting bones and misshapen stone.

The more you think along these lines, the more you will notice that the multitudes do not care for the senses of the words they speak – even less for the cumulative meanings of the words they string into propositions. You will discover how much more human speech, in practice, resembles grunting and bleating than actual language. Which is ironic, seeing as language is as inherent to every one of us as is the fact of our humanity, for the one is defined by the other. To call this missing the mark is to understate the sin and so miss the mark doubly. Contemplation is a rudimentary technique, not forgotten knowledge. Did I not say I feel like the Water Seller in the rain? Again, I do not force anyone to buy my water. I only ask that people stand up (*those fools!*) and if they're not at all interested in water, to at least get themselves out of the mud.

Layers of Silence

But I am aware that there are still people reading this (though many have likely left by this point) who are not convinced – sure, the metaphor checks out, but still: *it is just a metaphor!* Mine is not the kind of proposition to be allowed the luxury of easy acceptance. It is not attractive, it is not quite conventional, and what it reveals is not an upturned thumb to the preferences of the modern person. Ideological priority is allotted only to their unconditional encouragement. *It is only a metaphor!* one imagines the unconvinced protesting, *Nothing but an overindulgence in fancy; a linguistic jest, and so much empty babble!* One must not imagine the protestor as being at all aware of the irony when he says that the author is just toying with language. Although, I will not disagree with all of his accusations. I feel no more shame in my indulgence than indulgence in virtue deserves, in as far as we are the descendants of civilizations that have not villainized contemplation but in their darkest moments. Nor do I deny that I am *playing* with language in as far as play, be it physical, intellectual, or even spiritual, is functionally an effective method of learning. Play, like indulgence, is only bad when it is done ineffectively, which is to say when it is mishandled, misdirected, or misunderstood as the many things to which its semantic scope has granted resonance, and convention has degraded into literality. But then again, that too is just a metaphor.

I am aware that the enemy's lie in the opening chapters was built upon layers of untruth; I already said that the first step was the (successful) attempt to equivocate the abstract with the unreal. The second step was to extend that to metaphor. I am beginning to realize just how hard my task really is. I cannot hope to convince a man of the significance of a particular metaphor if he already believes all metaphor to be categorically void of any meaning applicable to the real world that could ever be as real as the world itself. There will always loom the suspicion that metaphor is below literality, a spinoff or a subsidiary to what is real – that it is uniformly not real, and so, something best reserved for out-of-touch philosophers or pretentious poets: for the domain of fancy one is expected to outgrow as one nears adulthood, as the questions associated with the curiosity of children become replaced by the silence associated with disinterested adults.

But that is just the thing. It is exactly where the problem lies, for questioning is in the essence of language. Just imagine what human language would be like without overt questions, and just how much communication would be lost without that hooked, dotted symbol; and then imagine communication without even the implicit questions suggested in affirmative phrases that imply an antecedent interrogative, such as a professor's propositions in a classroom, philosophical appeals to an audience, or even everyday talk in everyday households, and you will see what I mean. Imagine humanity that has never been touched by education, by philosophy, or even so much as a sincere *how has your day been?* Imagine the degree of knowledge we would have in such a world, and, so as to be consistent with the fantasy, try to describe it to me without assuming I would care to ask you about it.

The ideal way to silence a nation is to silence its questions. Once more, dictators come to my aid by exemplary means. In this same manner, the best way to silence humanity is to kill metaphor: curiosity regarding concept. To do away with inherited knowledge, to downplay the importance of new knowledge, to encourage a selective amnesia, and to inspire a silence presiding over all phenomena. To posit an adulthood that, not an upgrade to childhood, has been forged as the destroyer of childhood – ask no questions, and you will hear no lies; expect nothing for Christmas, and you will not believe in Santa Claus. But do you not find it at all disturbing when behavior associated with the beginning of life is regarded as inferior to behavior perfected in death? Dead metaphors are not just a fancy name. Like dying cells, they are a foretelling of the fate of the organism. It is the permanent desolation of language, and the ushering of the era of total silence.

A Predominantly Technical Discourse, Predominantly on Language

A Lesson in Language

The definition of language as man's primary tool for communication has taken hold of too many textbooks to be pardoned as the myth that it is – having become in scope similar to historical legends we still believe or popular theological maxims many profess, it is not an innocent fallacy, but a dangerous delusion. Being the iconoclast that I am, questioning the limitless reign of numbers in my first book, I am now inclined to question (and hope to reform!) the delimited reign of words as well.

To begin, I will first say that language is not a tool for communication.[8] In as far as the goal is communication, you will find language to be something between a subsidiary and a distraction. Many mammals can communicate just as well as humans do, and they have not the semblance of human language. Some make noises, some rely on what we have dubbed body-language for want of imagination, and most do a combination of the two. If we extend to birds, we will encounter species that can imitate human speech. And still, they are without language. The reader may find what I am about to say surprising, but the same goes for us humans. We are just as capable of communicating the essentials of the external world without so much as saying a word,[9] and, what's more, that is precisely what we do before our brains have developed the competence to handle something as nuanced as language. Syntax and semantics, including an expansive lexicon, are essential to language, but they are not

---

[8] In that communication is not its primary function.

[9] Paralinguistic cues play just as big a role in successful communication as spoken or written language. If you don't believe me, try shouting angrily at a stranger on the street, "I respect you, sir, and I consider you a productive member of society!" wile threatening him with your fist, and see just how much your semantic content influences his reaction.

essential to communication. In the case of the former, they are like the lens of a telescope; to the latter, they are as spectacles to a man with 20/20 vision. What use is syntax when you can simply grunt your message? For this paragraph, suffice it to say that man's primary tool for communication is not his language, but his voice. His secondary tool is his competence to gesture, and, lastly, his auxiliary tool is empathy.[10] We can use these three to communicate as animals do and to convey information of the same kind. Not only can we signal attraction and danger and annoyance between ourselves, but we also use such languageless expressions to communicate with animals attuned to them, such as dogs, which, though incapable of language, can readily understand a smile or a bent head or an angry shout.

Language is something which definition, according to its purpose, can be worded to denote a metaphysical vehicle. If the term *communication* must be used, then language is the means by which our thoughts communicate with our minds. It is how reality understood keeps in check with reality perceived. Language is the voice of reason. Yes, it travels on sound waves and it can rest on symbols, but it only ever originates, propagates, and dwells in the one thing that cannot be expressed without it – thought. Do not be confused by the necessity for the physical voice – whenever you talk to another person, it is really two minds hijacking the vocal folds to enact a telepathic request. Sound is merely an enabler.

The mind and its many manifestations were designed to adapt to their environment. Were the concept of thought a biological organism, a Darwinist might call this an offshoot of its instinct for self-propagation. Then again, there is no reason he (the Darwinist) should abstain from the privilege – Darwinism has not been constrained to biological reality for the better part of a century. Thought adapts to its environment, and, when thriving, far from contentedly enjoying its reign in isolation, it seeks to

---

[10] However you choose to define it.

spread further. If threatened, it does not retreat for long, but tries to readapt – like the pakicetus on its way to swallow Jonas, forming itself anew, once subdued, now emerging greater than ever.

As individual thought thrived through oral tradition, its major hurdle was a matter of physics, and its lifespan was restrained to the lifespan of those who knew it; in addition to the temporal handicap, its propagation was restrained by geography, for voice can only travel so far. For the longest time, if it were to transgress borders, thought had to rely on fragile and temporary mediators. And so, there appeared a new form, one independent of voice and geography and even time, and only contingent on code – as long as one knew the code, instead of learning individual thoughts as separate sets, one could potentially know all thoughts rendered in it by means of an epistemologically unitary set. As this happened, thought would hibernate on clay, stone, parchment, or papyrus[11]. Biological enthusiasts might enjoy this next bit. With the invention of the alphabet, language, the carrier of thought, the voice of reason, became analogous to microbes. Comprehensive reading is an infection of the mind (by another mind), that enters the body through the retina; given the right circumstances, it can penetrate the ear canal; the bacteria that carries it resides on letters – a rather filthy affair compared to a blank slate: no letters, no bacteria; covered eyes are safe from infection; and so is a sterile mind.

And for all its prosperity, language seeks more: reason must be known; thought will not exist but in the minds of men, and the minds of men will not tolerate a thoughtless existence. It is a symbiosis without which both perish. So what of those whose linguistic mechanism is, partially or entirely, permanently broken or, even if functional, we find it insufficient in one regard or another? Will the mind then remain silent? Certainly not. Where language will not suffice as such, regardless the cause, the world

---

[11] ...or dirt wood metal or skin – feel free to add more if I missed any.

will be translated by different means – thought will find a way, and reason will yet be reasonable, even if voiceless. Thought emerges as art, visual and musical, and this new adaptation of our subject has proven so potent that even men capable of speech admire it and use it either in lieu of language or in addition to language, so extensively as to form such strange amalgamations as poetry. Such impressive devices as sign language too, so that the minds of the voiceless can at last be voiced – and dare not scoff at the metaphor.

Mathematics does not stand apart from this either. No, a formula and a function are not sentences, I will concede there – however, as sign-language is to a deaf person, or runes are to people lacking letters, functions and formulas are a short-hand for what can be said in sentences but is just simple enough to be understood without them. For the voice of reason is a minimalist affair: syntax is not employed where mere semantics will suffice, and semantics will not overextend where symbol is enough. Saying *Hey!* to your friend is not a sentence, and graffiti is not literature. There are not many ways to interpret a mathematical equation, nor are there that many things that an interpreted mathematical equation can tell us by itself. It is only when language is involved that numbers begin to mean anything: such as when a place with two houses built at different times had at a prior point only one house, and earlier still it had zero houses, but there was never a point at which there were physically minus one houses, for there is not anything that can ever be less than nothing – *two minus one minus one minus one* alone has no meaning; or when the Golden Ratio is argued to apply to our concept of beauty provided we understand the metaphorical value of gold and have come to some agreement on the concept of beauty as a strictly visual symmetry – at which point we are back to the subject of words.

And so, one wonders: if such is the nature of language, and the origin of art is reason speaking without a linguistic carrier, then why must it be the case that both are regarded as but reason's illusory quasi-manifestations, to the extent where they are being further derided as reason's antithesis, on account of another facet, which, far from being reason's ideal representative, is instead among its simpler variants in the case of numbers, and no kind of relative whatsoever in the case of convention? My question is not rhetorical in retrospect, as I have answered it in my previous essay. For now, all that needs saying is that a spoken word is not a flick of the tongue, but an extension of the mind. And the sooner we come to treat it with the respect it deserves, the sooner we will be able to enact the archetype of the wizard curing the land of a curse, by the utterance of a spell, to remedy what started out as another utterance, but spoken by a malicious, ignorant, or misguided villain.

So the next time you find yourself thinking that language is one of those negligible facets of reality which we can comfortably brush off for it has been either replaced or proven unimportant or just one of those necessary annoyances in life in the same category as public transport, keep in mind that what you are really thinking about is the severing of your connection to reason: you are thinking about giving up proper thinking; about using a mudbath to clean yourself, throwing away the baby to save on bathwater, or straining a gnat to swallow a nutritious fish.

Language is the voice of reason. It exists to explain reality. Language is the only thing between mankind and the mute abysses of ignorance. We owe everything we have to our abilities to conceptualize and to speak. Without them, our ability to think would be more like a nightmare than anything else. Imagine a person who can (somehow) see everything but can focus on nothing, or a person who can focus on something but cannot single out anything. His safest, sanest choice would be to close his eyes. To open them would be an assault against himself.

Language begins with successful conceptualization. It then goes on to renew itself, to test itself, and to improve itself with further conceptualization. Concept is the core and the soul of language.

In order to see why it is so, we must survey language and determine its mechanisms. Not as an everyday practical part in the everyday lives of practical people, and certainly not as an ethnic phenomenon with its ethnic fallacies, but on that initial level that justifies linguistic science, in as far as it justifies the concept of language and the concept of science alike. I am talking about understanding, or language as the means by which reason is actualized.

If the reader is already convinced of what I have said so far, the reader should feel at liberty to skip to the end of this section, and go on to the less technical part that follows. The subject I proceed to explain here is mostly a response to (let us call it) conceptual hesitance. Then again, I predict that the majority of those who do read it will be of the camp that is already in agreement with my point on language. The others will have long left by now. And to be bluntly honest, that is how I prefer it.

The Abstract Cell

We are at all conscious instances exposed to phenomena of which the most salient are phenomena we perceive. Their salience, admittedly circularly, is determined by the fact of our perception, and this perception would not be called that if not for an active process making it distinct from its effective opposites. Its opposites, we should note, are proportional to the spectrum of sentience if looked upon in the negative direction, which finds its extreme in reflexive reaction, and is perfected only in such entities as have no sentience at all. On the other end of this same spectrum, we find, in fantastical discourse, persons with preternatural abilities, and, in naturalist discourse, people with very keen senses. Slightly below them is the person we would call the average person, and just below that are *emergent* persons (and do pardon the term I have used for infants if it offends you). Other than their personal agency, these entities differ in knowledge, their capability to gain knowledge, and their ability to utilize their senses to that end. From here, it is reasonable to conclude that perception is a process that, on the low end, is conditioned by sentience, and, on the high end, is closely related to a person's ability to know things – the more one knows, the more one is capable of perceiving, and the more one can perceive, the higher the likelihood that one should be able to learn. We could not have discovered bacteria had we not first perceived some aspect of them, nor could a student get a Ph.D. in bacteriology unless they could perceive many aspects of them. What's more, you could not even conceptualize bacteria unless you could first tell them apart from the rest of the world, in the sense that bacteria is not a virus or protoza, or the standard by which H. pilori and E. coli can be part of the same set but distinct from others. Therefore, to perceive something is to be able to tell it apart from everything else that is not it, and to establish non-arbitrary rules by which its instantiations can be it. And so, when, as a developing mind, you first begin to utilize your intellect, even if you cannot word it, you become aware not just of a jumble of reactions and desires, but a jumble of objects and events: you can tell apart round from square, food from object, object from agent, and agent with two legs from your single aunt's baby. We are still far from a fully-formed language system, but perception is a start.

Perception leads to the creation of sets. Sets organize meaning. The next step is the formation of concepts. The two must exist in tandem. Sets would be of little use to us if we could not render them as distinct semantic constructs. I say this because sets, which in the first draft I called semantic categories, are the intelligently organized amalgamations of perception; without anything to attest for the fact of their intelligent organization, there would be nothing to distinguish sets from perception's antonym of reflexive reaction. Consider, for example, that when observing an interaction suggesting a logical pattern, what we may on first sight judge to be *evidence* of categories for things that cause pleasure and things that cause pain, lacking concept, would be likelier to prove a set of behaviors in reaction to stimuli –

familiarized to varying extent, but not at all instances of intelligent organization one can reasonably regard as a case where distinct set of perceptions A is associated with distinct phenomenon B; the simplest explanation for the correlation between A and B is that of reaction A responding to stimulant B, irrespective of the alleged complexity of the observed behavior, which may imitate, but never instantiate semantics. In short, without concept, there can be no proof of category as a fact of intelligent perception. Fortunately, concepts do exist, and so we can know that what we do, whenever we assume we are trying to make sense of the world and the things in it, is in fact trying to make sense of the world and the things in it. Category organizes, and concept selects.

The two stand in a sense-relationship of intension and extension. To illustrate this relationship, imagine a set of things that are round and moderately hard and filled with air, that bounce on impact, with a circumference of 74.9 cm, and are primarily designed to be thrown in hoops. This is the concept of a basketball. Between it and the set, there are the intention and the extension of the word. The intension is the description I have written above; the extension are all of the potential basketballs you may see or imagine. We will define extension as all the things that a concept may cover, and intention as those requirements that something must meet if it is to qualify for the set. You may envision the interaction between set and concept as shown below:

Scheme: Example:

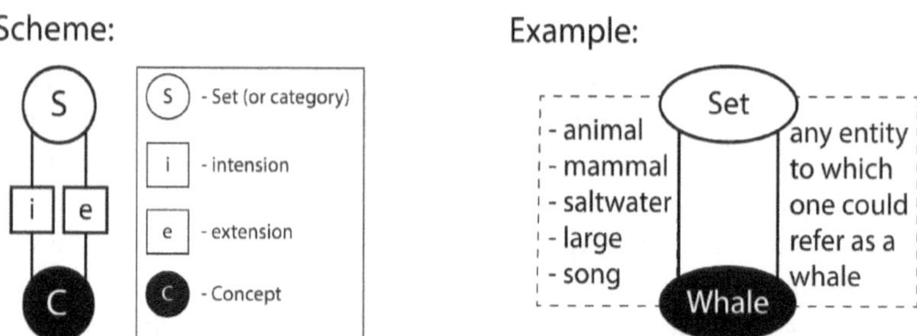

Fig. 1: the abstract cell: set, intension, extension, and concept. The example employs the colloquial sense of the word *whale*.

These should not be regarded as clear and strictly delimited sets of meaning, as the precise lexical equivalents of Russian nesting dolls, but, as the analogy is not entirely inapplicable, like Schrodinger's quantum dolls with attachment disorder: they can (and do) still nest, but it is hard to tell where, to what extent, and for how long – and yes, the comparison has reach, as measuring them tends to influence their position. A concept can pair with multiple sets, and a set can cover indefinitely many concepts, as long as it provides semantic material for the concepts to select.

The intension and extension of words are in constant flux as they are updated to keep in touch with reality. If we are to discover a small whale, or an extant specie that thrives exclusively in sweet water, the intension shown in fig. 1 will undergo serious alteration. If at one point a bird was any animal with wings, the perception of insects altered the avian intention to a *vertebrate* with wings. This new criterion ruled out flying insects and the occasional winged politician. The discovery of other flying vertebrates cemented the criterion of warm-blooded, and the perception of bats as distinct animals further altered the intension of the word to cover non-mammals. Of course, feathers, beak, and talons might have taken part in the equation at some earlier point. The above is not the etymology of *bird*; it is merely a hypothetical demonstration of the evolution of sense. The thing to take out of it is that intension widens, extension narrows, concepts become richer (and for the same reason less expansive), as the intellectual organization (or sets) of things blossoms into additional concepts by the newly engendered semantic relationships for the translation of the natural world.

This union between category and concept makes up the sense of words: it is the interaction between perception and recognition, including the perception and recognition of other sets and concepts. The semantic entity they form makes up the abstract element of word-meaning, since it is rooted in intersemantic relations between nonconcrete entities. Let us, for this reason, observe the proper way of understanding the meaning of *abstract*, and, by extension, what an *abstract meaning* really is. You will find that it is not nearly as vague, undefined, or as unreliable as the conceptual skeptic imagines it to be.

Concept, Object, Art

None of these are metaphysical claims. I theorize from an exclusively semantic point of view. My argument is about the relationship between abstract concepts and fundamental human belief,[12] not the nature of their existence (if they even do exist). That would be the realm of philosophy, or the way that philosophers approach the abstract. When a philosopher speaks of abstract objects, though he may also discuss what I have described above, the unique input in his field would be mostly what I have omitted in my text – whether abstract *objects* are real, in what way they might be real, under which category would certain non-material entities fall given the reality of abstract objects, etc. Though the two fields may overlap (and they often do), they differ in their points of interest: philosophy is associated (uniquely) with ontology, whereas the semanticist deals with epistemology – not existence, but linguistic perception, understanding, and the circumstances under which one can argue in favor or in opposition to either.

Something similar can be said about the use of the term in art. It is not entirely compatible with either the linguistic interest or the philosophical pursuit. Abstract art, according to the *Encyclopedia Britannica*,[13] can be also called "nonobjective" or "nonrepresentational art," and it is described as visual art in which the "portrayal of things from the visible world plays little or no part." Though it is somewhat resonant with the concept of metaphor, its lack of objectivity distances it from the semantic case.

---

[12] In the sense of intellectual convictions;

[13] As I am not at all qualified in the history of art, I have decided to reference an elementary, neutral, and noncontroversial source on the subject;

Semantics is the study of meaning. Therefore, it is necessary that the concept under study has a distinct meaning, independent from the speaker's input. To be fair, there is plenty of abstract art in the world that is not meaningless, and the entry does make light of the argument that all art is, in some sense, abstract: "Remember that a picture... is essentially a flat surface covered with colours assembled in a certain order" (Denis) – which I seem to have argued elsewhere before knowing it.[14] However, the fact that abstract art covers nonobjective art as well, or art with no meaning other than what its beholder may assign to it, remains a point of incompatibility between semantics and art that cannot be ignored. So, if the reader feels obliged to liken abstract concepts to abstract art, he should think Picasso – not Pollock. Nobody has two eyes on the same side of their face, but they are certainly eyes and it certainly is a face. Remember: in semantics, sense is essential.

Semantics must rely on the premise of an objective meaning, by which variations of understanding can be compared, and from which a base notion may be derived – else, it would be too informal to count as any kind of science outside of a statistic on spoken whim. To the relativist: I do not suppose you would say that, given the relativity of the concept of legacy, a person that estimates Shakespeare's canon as a doorstop is objectively no less correct on the subject of the Bard's legacy than a person who teaches a college course on the Swan of Avon. Do note that statistics will not swing the validity of that argument either way. Majority vote has no claim on language purified from mob rule.

Language is rooted in meaning – for all purposes, language and meaning are one and the same. Meaning and understanding are also interwoven – wherever you have understanding, there must

---

[14] "'Now, in the case of the artist, that is, he who captures reality, we speak of true fictions – reality made manifest in a form in which it does not usually manifest. The coronation of Napoleon was never a splash of paint on canvas, but Jacques-Louis David made a splash of paint on canvas become The Coronation of Napoleon'" (*The Playwright* 235).

also be meaning, and meaning would mean nothing unless it has been understood. If you, a chemist, showed me the structure of a chemical substance, and I said *This means nothing to me*, you would tell me *That's because you don't understand it*. Conversely, if I could catch some distant memory of having seen the formula in high school, I just might say what it means as far as I understand it, likely with an accuracy slightly shy of a *D-*. The degree of understanding depends, after all, on the person's qualification to recognize meaning – it is only the factuality of meaning that is objective, in that, if there were none of it in your chemical formula, you would not understand it either (for there would be nothing to understand). Understanding testifies for meaning, and meaning enables understanding.

But there is one other observation to be made regarding the paragraphs above: in spite of the differences to which I have pointed, the three senses of abstract concept, object, and art, do share a similarity beyond the lexical, which in turn accounts for the lexical similarity: they all deal in phenomena which sense cannot be derived by a simple glance – not a subject of the senses, abstract meaning is not subjected to the senses, and so, far from the comfort of external assertion, abstract meaning relies on the individual free will: not in the subjective sense to determine it, but in the volitional intellectual sense to find it; by which the observer must decide to look for it, and he must labor for it – labor for the specific meaning, do note, amidst a sea not of clearly delimited meanings, such as the comfort of the five senses allows, but among a deluge of senses of which only a select few can ever be valid. Studying the abstract is always an adventure, and, not an epic to be diminished by the armchair where it is begotten (if the adventurer is ever so lucky to own an armchair), it is an adventure so confined physically that it is in every other regard a journey through an indefinite scape of riveting twists and terrible bores; pretention not presenting an uncommon hazard, the study of the abstract is an adventure that takes its hero on a journey through the realms of history, argument, logic, sense, and observation, none of which can be accessed but through the cranial singularity of the human mind.

<u>Unreal, Immaterial, Intangible</u>

So let us first consider what it really means to speak of the immaterial and of the intangible. Otherwise, materialist bias will have nullified any attempt to discuss abstract meaning before we have gotten halfway through with the argument. I stand no chance of arguing for the validity of metaphor, let alone a metaphor with such a moral clout as universal brotherhood, if my reader writes off metaphor on account that he cannot touch it. But though the concepts I discuss are immaterial, to call them unreal is to speak in offense of existence itself – and I say this without a shred of ontological stipulation beyond the two core ontological stipulations, namely that we all exist, and that we have the (existing) minds to understand that we really do. Perhaps the following paragraphs will make that clear – I repeat, without a shred of ontological stipulation beyond the fundamental.

The immaterial realm should be easy to grasp, as a definition, since all it contains is, by the word's meaning, whatever is not material – you cannot see it hear it touch it smell it or feel it, search as you might, technology notwithstanding, and so not for want of effort, but for its inherent intangibility. Likewise, the intangible is merely all that is not tangible. According to the *Merriam-Webster* dictionary, it is, by proxy, that which is not "(1a) capable of being perceived by the senses, especially by the sense of touch" and, on occasion, it can be synonymous with *immaterial* (1b). And yet, the two words are not interchangeable. For instance, it is a largely agreed upon proposition that intellect is immaterial, but to say that somebody's intellect is intangible means something else entirely. In the same source, one definition of the word *tangible* is of something "capable of being precisely identified or realized by the mind" (2). The offered example of the word in use is "her grief was *tangible*." In that sense, an immaterial referent may acquire a tangibility, which makes for a seemingly contradictory disagreement with the former synonymy. It would be as if to say that, though we agree that intellect is universally intangible, the intellect of a specific person may not be intangible, and somehow remain innocent of nonsense. I say *seemingly*, because what we are really witnessing is a case of polysemy in the definitions of tangibility: though the forms are identical in appearance, they have two separate meanings: tangible₁ is the original sense, historically derived from Latin *tangent* meaning *touching* (Skeat 541) and tangible₂ is its conventionalized metaphor roughly meaning *touchable by mind*, or *comprehensible*. In this light, the contrast between the two is not quite as bizarre as it may initially seem, as the sense-relation depends on the form; more importantly, it helps to specify the difference between the concept of the immaterial and the concept of the intangible: the former is a binary category, and the latter is a relational attribute.

The category of materiality tells us what something is made of; the way that a brick house is made of brick, and so you would not call a wooden house a brick house nor would you call a brick house susceptible to wolf attacks;[15] something can be either made of matter, and therefore material, or it is not of matter, i.e. it is immaterial. There is no object that can be two thirds material or about one and a half quarters immaterial. The literary value of James Joyce's *Finnegan's Wake* is immaterial, and there is no doubt that it always will be. We may also call it intangible, and we would remain in the right in the sense that we cannot physically touch it. The printed copy on the shelf in the bookstore is, of course, material. There can be no doubt about that either. Nor can there be any doubt that, being a predominately paper construct, the printed copy is perfectly

---

[15] This is a simplified analogy. Brick houses are not made exclusively of brick. But to call one a wooden house because it has oaken doorframes would tank the real estate market.

tangible. Choosing to describe something as either, however, determines which additional sense will be added to this shared meaning – the conceptual highlight unique to each epithet.

Tangibility denotes our ability to perceive something with the senses (originally touch), which contingency on persons has resulted in the conceptual license to relativize the concept into a second, narrower sense that has enabled its scalability. For most of us, the literary meaning of *Finnegan's Wake* is as intangible as it is immaterial. To quote James Joyce himself, "(bababadalghara-ghtakamminarronnkonnbronntonnerronntuonnthunntrovarrhou-nawnskawnt-oohoohoordenenthur-nuk!) of a once wallstrait oldparr is retaled early in bed and later on life…"[16] It is not so, however, to the scholar who has studied it. For him, it certainly is tangible. Although something is either material or immaterial, in which sense it cannot vary, whether it is also tangible or intangible is susceptible to variation from one speaker to another.

So when we say that something is immaterial, we speak of its substance, namely the lack of matter defining its existence. It is a statement about the object. When we say that something is intangible$_1$ what we really mean is that it is not subject to the senses, which, though often so due to its immaterial character, is a statement not about the object in isolation, but about the relation between the object and the speaker (or the object and mankind), which ensuing cognitive extrapolation has allowed for tangibility$_2$, which, to the five senses, being the prime instruments of tangibility, adds mind as the sixth. According to the semantic evidence, tangibility$_2$ can overrule an intangibility if the mind allows it.

In conclusion, though the two terms (immaterial and intangible) can be identical in regards to substance, they differ in perspective – one being an objective category of the outside world, and the other a relation of the outside world to the observer, be it a general or a specific observer, liable to subjective modification.

---

[16] No, that is not a misprint.

What usually comes up in discussions like these is mankind's exclusive ability to call forth the immaterial world. This is supposed to invalidate abstract concepts as a delusion of the only specie intelligent enough to have any. What is not so frequently the case is that people recognize that reality is not so. The intangible is very much a feature of animal communication. When a bird screeches to signal danger to its flock, what it signals is not the specific kind of threat it has perceived: a cougar or a snake or a man with malicious intent – nor does it necessarily signal threat, for the mere semblance of threat can also provoke the reaction. It is instead an expression of the *conviction* of danger: an intangible experience with a potential determinate cause in the outside world, but no specific referent entailed in the content of the message itself. The thing about animal communication is precisely their lack of specific reference, which makes the concepts they try to signal intangible in both senses: the concepts we read in their reactions, being expressions of conviction, as opposed to some state of affairs, are immaterial, which makes them intangible$_1$, and since they (the animals) have no intellectual understanding of them, they are also intangible$_2$. Whenever animalkind appears to approximate (the semblance of) humanlike communication is at those instances when they do (appear to) understand a specific reference, i.e. when they have been trained to act as if they do: a dog answering to the utterance of its name, an ape signing *snack* when it wants one, or a parrot calling you *friend!*[17] The same applies to mankind in the early stages of our development, before language has begun to manifest our gift of reason. The babbling of babies is not considered speech, even when they do happen to get something right. It is the use of a specific referent that determines the development of language.

---

[17] Though it (clearly) has no concept of friendship, your pet would not have learned the word from you unless it saw you as one. Regardless, it does not call you friend because it considers you its friend, but because you have taught it to utter those particular sounds.

This reference, in the totality of cases with which I have been acquainted, is a reference to a tangible piece of reality: most commonly material, and always understood.

So it is not referential intangibility that imposes itself on nature, and is therefore liable to accusations of unnaturalness, but the opposite: intangibility is the default, and it is tangibility that *infiltrates*, to use an expression of imposition, the natural order of prompt and reaction. There is no semantic substance in the hissing of a cat, which, expressing frustration, wills to be left alone; just as there is no shrillness in the text message *leave me alone*, though its semantic abundance is rivaled only by its extra-semantic implications. Language does not merely seek to express, but to explain. And it can only explain things from the assumption of meaning – else, there would be nothing to explain. This ability is confirmed, let us call it *the rite of speech* as a parallel to a rite of passage, in the ability of language to code the $tangible_1$. It is a reasonable check. The first step to trusting a system for the understanding of reality is to test the system on a piece of reality that can be easily verified. The moment you have proven yourself capable of naming the things we can all see, you have proven yourself capable of language: you explain things, and we can all agree on them. If, to the languageless, $tangible_1$ is $intangible_2$, people of the same language can understand it for both $tangible_1$ and $tangible_2$.

So with this in mind, we should next consider the relationship between the immateriality of concept and other immaterial concepts: when human language, recognized by its capability to call forth the physical world, or its maturation from expressions of the intangible to subject matter associated with the $tangible_1$, turns again to the intangible, only this time, with the intent of making specific references out of $intangible_1$: instead of a baby babbling happily because she is happy, an adult saying that she is happy, asking others if they are happy, and discussing what she believes it means to be happy – keep in mind, uttering the kind of content capable not only to express a state of emotion, as does the chirping of a bird or a dog's wagging of the tail, but to recognize, pinpoint, and to explain, just as one does for entities in the material world.

These are concepts we understand exclusively by their sense, their sense being in the interaction between organized meaning and selected meaning, alongside other resonant bits of organized or selected meanings, which we discussed earlier in the book. They differ from the concrete world in that they are not tangible$_1$, but they differ from the rest of the intangible world in that they are sensible. They have meaning. Naturally, this meaning cannot be derived by means quite as simple as the workings of the five senses, however, it is for this reason that it is a meaning far richer in content than the meanings we derive for objects that can boast of the material privilege. They do exist, in as far as they are perceivable in the same setting as tangible$_1$. If we say *His love for his country has never been a subject of dispute*, we very clearly speak of things we have perceived in the material world: love, country, subject, dispute, a foreignness to time... they are all real, though none of them are tangible$_1$. We cannot confirm what we mean by them the way we can confirm what we mean by the words ball or bowl or bull. They are not quite as tangible$_2$ and they are not at all tangible$_1$. It is for this reason that their meanings are often subjects of debate. *What is a country? What is love? What is never?* These are concepts which meanings we must map on our own; our only means of navigating the cognitive space is sense: the way our conceptualizations measure up to our observations.

And this is the wealth of abstract concepts – they are so rich in meaning, that we can all agree on them in a fundamental sense (for example, that one's love for one's country one does not manifest by destroying one's country), and we can disagree on them in every other sense, for instance, whether one's love for one's country manifests as a centralized rule to ensure the common good, or a strong private sector to ensure the prevention of centralized rule. The following debate on the subject, yelling excluded, is how we go about determining what it means to love one's country – we test each concept against what we observe in practice; and we test it against other concepts, such as justice, or purpose, or dignity. We should not be deterred by the fuzziness of abstract concepts. On the contrary, we should embrace it. Because accepting the multitudes of possible definitions and the multitudes of opposing definitions is the beginning of understanding; it is the point at which the rite of language, being a rite of passage, ushers in the transformative maturity for which it exists; adulthood will not linger in the black-and-white world of kids, of addition and subtraction and right and wrong determined by a checkmark, dabbling in the fundamentals of reading and writing and dismissing knowledge at the sound of the school bell. No, adulthood tames the wilderness, builds bridges, settles the plains, traverses the mountains, lands on the moon, and it yearns for the sky. It is all in the name of understanding. Yes, adulthood also makes wars, exploits the destitute, and ruins nature. But that is a product not of understanding, but of childishness, of simplicity, of hubris... it is not real adulthood, but a big child having faked his way through the rite of language. It is the titular problem. And by now you should be able to guess the solution.

Abstract Misgivings

It has to do with the evolution of language. I do not mean a Darwinian evolution across the many, now-extinct, mysterious, fascinating species as which we began before we evolved into just another species, but the evolution of the lexicon as understood on a personal conceptual model. There can be no tangible evidence for this kind of theory except for the evidence of concept, which is, of course, not at all *hard* evidence. But I should note that the same goes for just about any linguistic speculation. Nor is this restrained to the study of language – historians are just as prone to it, and some natural scientists have the same problem. It is difficult to offer firm evidence when no hard evidence exists. But the silver lining in the study of conceptual evolution is that its

provability is mainly conceptual itself, and so is the belief in it –
so, at the very least, it is consistently speculative, if not
consistently provable.

A quick summary of the argument so far goes that, if human
language is a process initially made distinct by direct references
to the tangible world, but in so doing it creates a link between the
material world and the immaterial realm of concept, then the
function of language is one of conceptualization, or of creating
categories by which the world of the senses becomes integrated
into the world of sense. Language immaterializes the material
world: it lifts a meaningless world into a world of meaning; it
makes tangible$_1$ into tangible$_2$. In regards to abstract concepts, the
part of the world that is being synthesized into tangible$_2$ begins as
intangible$_1$.[18] This might rub some materialists the wrong way.
Hence the chapter.

The debate between materialists and non-materialists has been
raging on for a time which span I cannot estimate without
underestimating it, but I can say with confidence that the length
of the battle has not been due to powerful wits, but to relentless
zealots. Regardless, however many disagreements there may be
on the subject, the strong materialist position cannot be the case
for all immaterial instantiations. Hallucination is not present as
matter, though it does appear to the senses. Anxiety is not
material either, but you can certainly feel it. The two are
perfectly tangible in the general sense of tangible$_1$ for they are
known to the senses attuned to the material world. A possible
objection to this could be that the fact of our perception proves
these experiences (and those like them) to be material after all,
but it is not a very good objection, considering it fails to address
the necessity of their factual absence from the material world to

---

[18] As for what happens with intangible$_2$, I am afraid we have no way of
knowing – otherwise it would not be wholly intangible$_2$, at which point
it is but a subset of tangible$_2$.

qualify them as the phenomena as which we recognize them. After all, my parasomniac sighting of a giant huskie was not a magical huskie, appearing next to my bed in the split-second before it vanished, as do the demons of other men's nightmares do for them, but a projection of my mind. Hallucinations are by definition not material, and the fact that we recognize them for hallucinations – phantasms with no bearing on the physical world in spite of their fleeting appearance in it – is proof of their immateriality. Otherwise, they might as well be real entities that do pop in and out of existence, and we would have no reason to think of them as anything else. Hallucination must be, by definition, something not present in the material world that we nonetheless perceive with senses meant to perceive materiality. Whatever chemical processes occur in our brains to mark them as distinct experiences are as the letter a child may write to Santa Claus – though everything about the letter is part of the material universe of discourse, a concrete fact of reality, from the ink and the paper and the present being demanded of the charitable saint, which will, should the parents so decide, indeed appear beneath the Christmas tree, the bearded mascot is himself not. A similar argument can be made to establish the experience of anxiety as an immaterial phenomenon, and I welcome the reader to try it. So I do not think that the immaterial realm should be conceptually denied on materialist grounds for its apparent foreignness to the senses. As long as hallucinations can be called hallucinations and unique experiences can be called unique experiences, so should abstract concepts be accepted, if nothing else, as just valid enough to have some bearing on the real world, as do concepts regarding tangible$_1$, by which concept may be called what it is – even under materialist dogma.

I find it odd when I hear people assert that the scope of tangible$_2$, which we could also call real, meaningful, or accessible to human comprehension, in regards to the immaterial, is valid only to the extent that we can see it replicated in the natural world. They believe that such concepts as the concept of fear, as evidenced in a screeching bird, are valid in spite of their apparent immateriality, whereas immaterial concepts to which experience animalkind is silent, must be, given their absence from nature, not valid. Fair enough. Fear is real, for we see it all over – courage is not, for the lion's courage is merely human poeticism; attraction is as real as any other behavior we observe in animals – love is not, because cartoon animals do not count; senseless babbling is real, for it has an equivalent in many mammals (and some birds) – scientific inquiry, however, is just an adult imitation of senseless babbling. There are people who really do believe that our standard for what may constitute tangible$_2$ for intangible$_1$ should be creatures that cannot make tangible$_2$ even out of tangible$_1$.

Because so are tangible things like laughter or play or work or food or even people, immaterial in that they are mere concepts until they have been actualized in the material world – factual laughter and factual play and factual people – laughing and playing and doing humanly things. Note that for each material instantiation of a given object in the world, say, the instantiation of meat or beef or steak, its immaterial counterpart either exists as concept or it is created on the spot: whatever happens in the real world, even of the completely material kind, takes share in immaterial reality when it has been observed, considered, catalogued, or in some way communicated by a sentient entity – in such a dynamic that, upon its observation, the subject in question becomes without deviation a partaker in the immaterial realm by virtue of its established status as concept. It is the quality of tangibility$_2$ that allows us to understand things that are tangible$_1$ – they must possess the former before the question of their candidacy for the latter ever comes up.

If it were tangibility$_1$ that determines not just an aspect of sense, but meaning altogether, then we would be in a twofold trouble regarding what may and may not be known: if man's ability to conceptualize includes a conversion of tangible$_1$ into tangible$_2$, then, our understanding of tangible$_1$ would be just as meaningless as that of the intangible, seeing as tangible₂ is a part of intangible₁ in so far as tangible₂ presupposes the agency of the mind, which is commonly understood to refer to an immaterial phenomenon (to the extent that strict materialists deny the concept altogether); the other problem in denying that the intangible can have meaning is the subjectivity that gives the lexeme its specific sense, by which to argue that the intangible is either meaningless or of a meaning beyond the reach of the minds of men is to make a personal sketch and call it an epistemological atlas – you have no more right to assert it with confidence than anyone else, which makes for an ironic outcome in that it is often the people who hold themselves to be the champions of objective reality that are (in reality) just seeking to impose their own take on a concept defined by its relativity. You do not get to say what is tangible₂ and what is not any more than anyone else. For all you know, they are not deluded for believing in it, but it is you who fails to understand it.

Some here might call forth a correction to the former course, and hold that it is not zoology but neurology that determines the validity (or invalidity) of concepts, and, as such, we call real not those concepts which we observe among animals alone, but those concepts which evocation leaves a measurable imprint in the nervous system, and only in the sense (or extent) to which they are compatible with the nature of the imprint. But let us not fool ourselves. We cannot measure anything in the brain (or anywhere else) unless we have an idea of measurement and an idea of something to measure before we start. Regardless of the technology we intend to use to that end, the ideas we qualify as either measurable or unreal are no more present in the brain (or anywhere else in the material world) than the idea of calculation is present in the circuitry of a calculator. The engravings on a mechanical disk are to the mechanical disk no more tangible₂ for their tangibility₁ than whatever happens in our nervous system is tangible₂ to the nervous system itself – the physical tangibility of measured phenomena does nothing to make them comprehensible to just any agent. Though believable at a glance, it simply cannot be the case that tangible$_2$ is a product of tangible$_1$, but the opposite: it is tangible$_2$ that determines tangible$_1$.

There really is no reason to deny the validity of abstract concepts. Communication of immaterial phenomena is not even exclusive to mankind, so it can hardly be written off as the product of human blundering imagination in contrast to the rationality of non-rational species. Tangibility$_1$ does not substitute reality. The man who thought he saw a demon upon waking up, the bird that screams at the sudden swaying of a nearby branch, and the baby babbling happily because that is how she feels, are all partaking in the experience of the intangible – of hallucination, of conviction, of joy... but it is only the rational human capable of language who can validate these experiences for what they are. Not a senseless repetition of a syllable, not an invisible carnivore disguised as a gust of wind, nor a weightless demon floating above your bed just long enough to let you know that it likes watching you sleep[19]... but a manifestation of emotion, a spontaneous event in nature, and a fluke of the brain.

The distinction between perceived phenomena and the concepts as which we understand them to be (as opposed to the concepts which we know they are not) will never have existed if not for the validating power of language: if not for the immaterial, intangible universe of discourse knowable but to the human mind – a realm of concept, thought, and language; none of which are meaningless, for they all possess some degree of tangibility$_2$. We owe all of our knowledge, of the material world and the immaterial world alike, to the conviction that we have the privilege to tap into the latter.

---

[19] These are called hypnopompic hallucinations by the way; they are the highbrow version of parasomnia.

If you dragged your fist across your keyboard, the result would be, semantically, nothing worth mentioning. If you then, however, decided that the jumble of letters you have thus created is the name of a warrior nation in your fantasy novel, though it will not automatically become something worth reading, it will have acquired some semblance of semantics. It will have changed from nothing worth talking about to something that can at least be talked about. Similarly, if you drew a vertical line with a semicircle curving to the left attached to its bottom half, and, to the right, you drew a full circle of about the same size, and further right you drew a semi-circle bulging to the left, attached to the upper half of a vertical line, you would get a relatively unaesthetic linear structure. You might notice, however, as you observe your creation, that you have drawn the letters that make up the word *dog*. Note, these are not just the letters of the word, but also the word itself – not a meaning that is a group of lines arranged in a certain order, but a four-legged, domesticated, carnivorous mammal. Had we maintained the propensity for awe by which one's early childhood is so well-attuned to miracle by the time we got to learn to read and write, we ought to have marveled at this fact as if it were magic. Stranger still would be how, if you saw that same arrangement of letters elsewhere, though it would not be the same instance of that arrangement, and though it could differ significantly from the first in appearance, it too would say *dog* and it too would mean a four-legged carnivorous mammal we consider an ideal pet. It gets even weirder once you factor in the existence of that same word but in different languages. They are all different instantiations, but, in the right context, they are all the same thing. They are many, and yet, without deviation, they stand for the one. In fantasy, written words would be the avatars of a magical entity; in science fiction, written words would be the drones of an alien hive mind. If they were people in the real world, they would be political activists.

This is because the meaning of words does not reside within the words themselves, i.e. their form, but somewhere outside. If a word is to have meaning, it must point to something other than the sounds or letters that make it up. This is true of all things that have meaning. To illustrate, a road sign can only mean anything as long as it points to something else: sometimes, it points to a fact of geography, and sometimes it points to the law, but it never points to *nothing other than the attention it draws to itself*, except for cases of abandoned streets or lawless roads. On that note, we can tell apart words from random doodles, even in extinct languages which meanings we do not understand, by the fact that we can recognize those scribbles as pointing to something else, though we have trouble determining what that particular something really is.

Which leads us to my next point: if the abstractions of category and concept are to have any claim to anything definite, they must be paired with something concrete. Otherwise, any random string of sounds could be assumed to call to any random sets of perceptions, and language would be none the richer for it. As a matter of fact, that has always been the case – there are multitudes of noises one can produce that could, in theory, correspond to multitudes of senses, but we do not consider them parts of language when we hear them. If we are in the presence of a person who utters such gibberish, we assume either a lack of seriousness or aphasia, not neologism. Therefore, it is necessary for language that words have a conceptual anchor in which to direct the meaning selected by the concept. The example I gave above of the conceptual evolution of birds only works because of the concreteness of such things as birds and vertebrates and warm-blooded animals. You would not be able to speak of *living things that fly* if you could not even imagine flying living things. A quick way to confirm this is to observe that, if there is such a thing as we have no way of perceiving, we do not have a word for that particular thing, nor can we make one up without simulating its invitation into the perceptive field; conversely, if we can perceive it, physically or with the mind, we either have a word for it, or we are at least capable of making a word for it. So in order to get a word, we need two things: an agreed upon arrangement of sounds or scribbles denoting a concept, called a wordform, and a direction for this arrangement to something outside their existence as mere sounds or scribbles, by which our concept can be linked to reality (even if only conceptually). This is why, if our semantic cell is to ever form a functional semantic tissue, it must be linked to a third element, to which we *refer* as reference.

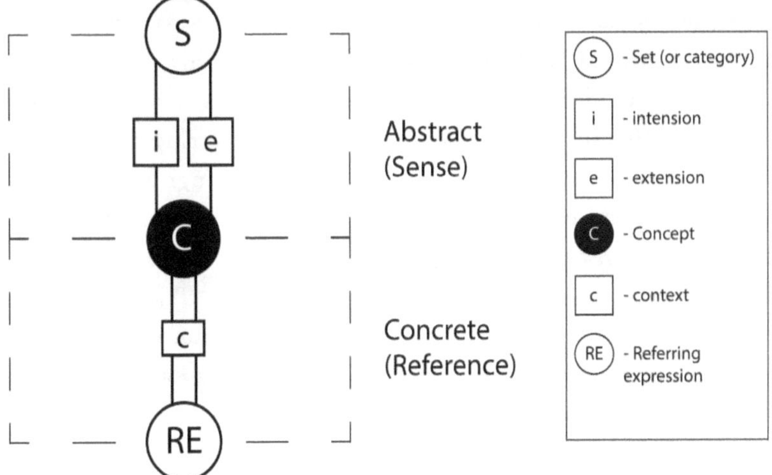

Fig. 2: The interaction between set, concept, and reference.

Let us consider a set of things you would not do for love. The intention would be something like *deed, not acceptable, personal decision.* The extension would be all of the things this covers, and *that* would constitute the concept. Semantically, it checks out. What would you not do for love? *That.* And you would be correct. *That* calls back to the set of unacceptable deeds. However, language would not be quite what it is if we had left it at *that*. This is why language relies on the existence of the lexicon.

We have established that meaning, once selected, must also be directed if it is to make up what we recognize as a word. Whatever our concept, it must be singled out in some way, either as a distinct lexeme[20] or as a thing in the world – think of pointing to an object or a picture of an object or some other manifestation of it and saying *that!* Now, think of the same act, but without the luxury of either proximity or a clear line of sight. Imagine that you could point at things with language. Next, realize that we do this already. If we speak of dogs, we have pointed to a set of all dogs; if we speak of a particular dog, we have pointed to that particular dog by saying its name or having singled it out from the rest of its species with a defining particle. This kind of expression is called a referring expression, the instance a reference, and the object it singles out is its referent. It is an unambiguous and omnipresent iteration of *that*. A reference can be general if it refers to a wider set, and specific, if it refers to a singled out entity or event. There is some discussion to be had on the subject, disagreements of definition and controversies of scope, but I do not think they are important for this particular discussion.

For now, let us consider the importance of context in the interaction between reference[21] and concept. You could not hope to refer to something unless the context were such that this something is *there*, wherever *there* may be, in the outside world or in the mind of the speaker, *somewhere you can point* all the same; this context could be something in one's external surroundings, the lexicon, a part of history, a previous line of speech, or some kind of idiomatic construct if it is *that of which we do not speak*.

------

[20] a word, as recognized in the dictionary;
[21] In most instances, *reference* and *referring expressions* can be used interchangeably. I will mostly use reference for brevity.

Wherever you locate your referent, the context must allow its distinction. For just as concept communicates with category by means of intension and extension,[22] so does concept communicate with reference by means of context.

Reference works as a kind of a tether outside concept, and context is the line that connects them. Together with the concept, the referring expression makes up the concrete end of the word, which is its *evocation* of a part of the world. Just as, paired with the set, concept makes up the abstract part of a word, which is the *invitation* of a part of the world into the mind. And so, when the intension is a walled-in construction in which people live, and the extension covers all possible houses, the concept of house manifests in language only when there is such a thing as a house of which the speaker is aware given the context: be it built, painted on canvas, or imagined, it is in any case a house, and a house to which the speaker is pointing: the house in which he lives, the archetype of all houses, a sub-archetype thereof, or a metaphor – it has been conceptualized and contextualized. It is somewhere outside of language, and it is being brought into language through the context of its utilization.

And there you have the cellular structure of words. A word begins with the perception of phenomena, rendered into sets, the proto-stage of semantic organization; it is determined by intension and extension, a set of selected meanings, and contextualized into an instance of reference. In the middle of it all stands concept to attest for both directions, in and out of the world of the senses and the world of sense. The product is the agreed-upon wordform as which we recognize the word.

---

[22] Remember, extension is a set of all the potential referents; assumed, but nonspecific and unactualized.

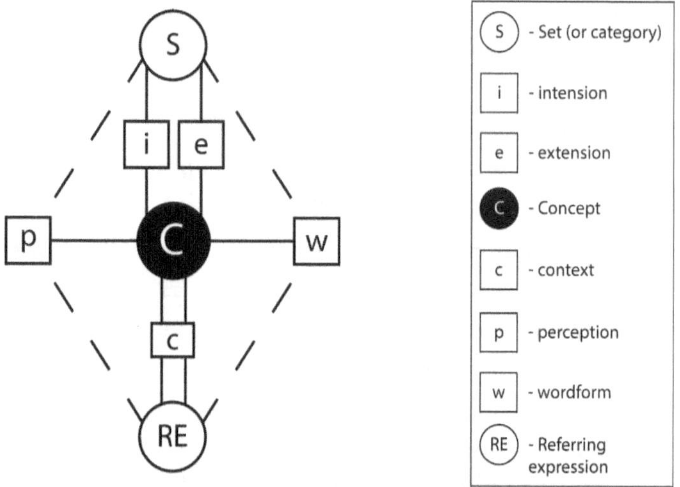

Fig. 3: The semantic process, from perception to wordform.

In this model, a word is really an instance of codified category, or an applied piece of perception. A change in one results in a change in all the others. What we understand by word meaning is really this interaction between sense and reference that arbiters the process by which the perception of distinct phenomena becomes associated with wordform.

Language is all about interpretation and pointing to things. So *that* is certainly vague without context, but if your lover accused you that "sooner or later you'll be screwing around", *that* is not at all vague when you tell her that you "won't do *that!*" (Steinman, "I'd Do Anything for Love"). But in case you are presented with further hypothetical scenarios, with the possible mentioning of what sounds like holy water, you might want to consider the ambiguity of the context before answering. Keep in mind, these are Schrodinger's quantum dolls. They will nest anywhere.

I chose the metaphor of the living cell, which I built up to the functional structure of tissue, for the reason that it is a metaphor of a living thing. The formation of word-meaning is as living a process in the mind as any living process is in biology. It has all the marks of living tissue, barring materiality: it is definite but susceptible to change, it is refined through time, and its ambition is to prolong itself by fitness, as the opposite is to perish through obsolescence. Moreover, as sense and the conceptual processes keep each other alive, the metaphor of the cell resonates with the concept of symbiosis. Ergo, the metaphor of a living structure – a *healthy* living structure.

All parts play into one another, and they are in all valid uses compatible with one another. If the context allows the connection between concept and reference, then the referent is also compatible with the set of things covered by the concept (the extension), and it has the sufficient characteristics to be regarded as a representative of the word (its intension). If you want to get poetic with it, you might notice that fig. 3 somewhat resembles a frontal view of the human eye. That was only mostly deliberate. After all, language is a facet of perception. But if you have good imagination, you might notice a slight resemblance between the sketch in fig. 2 and a technical sketch of an electric current. The similarity here is that all parts must be connected for the current to function. Concept is the diode that lets us know it works.

An interruption along any part of the conductors leads to no electricity at all. Eliminate sets, and you get a speaker unaware that there even is such a thing as meaning in the words he utters; he selects a sense randomly, and uses it to signify whatever – they may as well be shouting gibberish. If some set remains, but it is weakened or defective, the result would be similar but slightly subtler in its senselessness; think of a teenager using *literally* as an intensifier or *like* without intending to denote preference or comparison. There is no such thing as a semantic arrangement for these words; they are practical before meaningful, for there are no sensible rules to determine their use. *Like, you're literally killing me!* An interruption in the conceptual link would be an inability to select meaning. Indeed, some category does exist, but there is nothing to link it to a proper referent. It is just a jumble of spoken senses that amount to nothing. This is the ineloquent man using *that* and *the thing* to point to *that thing* which he is not quite sure he knows what it is himself. A discontinuity in reference would be what one sees in a practicing philosopher who is trying to describe things that are to him not quite as clear as he thinks. Think of a drug abuser who speaks of spiritual enlightenment; he does have an inkling of its intension and an extension of what could potentially stand for that word, and he can select some sense to signify an unburdened mind, although, as he directs this meaning not to awareness, but to stupor, the line of context is broken, and the conceptual diode goes out; there is no current, and the entirety of the structure is proven ineffective.

Any and all misunderstandings in human language can be traced to a defect somewhere along the sketch. This essay would be much shorter if semantic cells were universally functional. Alas, things are not so. There is confusion all around, and the clouds of mystery thicken. I cannot overemphasize the implications of this in practice. The most evident example is that of disputed reference: is it a bird or a plane, is it friendship or business, is it brave satire or a tasteless farce? But it is not the fact of dispute itself that worries me – at least not exclusively. What worries me is that people are either oblivious of the problems arising out of such misunderstanding, or, having been made aware of them, they are trying to renounce language altogether.

I will briefly call to attention the misunderstanding in which referential variety accounts for conflict in concept. People's definitions of the things they perceive are only as developed as the things they have been given the chance to perceive. A child soldier born and raised in a land where juvenile soldiery is a thing will likely have had no chance to develop a category for the virtue of mercy; if they happen to witness mercy, the concept they develop will be one of weakness, stupidity, or anomaly. Civilization is stupidity to a savage, just as a foreign culture is savagery to a chauvinist. A person from an abusive background might conceptualize abuse as love, and a person conventionally described as spoiled might conceptualize love as abuse. Even in phenomena within the material world, inherently unaffected by philosophy or nurture, such misunderstanding can (and does) arise, as conceptualization is inseparable from perception, which diversity and contingencies cannot be significantly altered by materiality. The reader has likely heard of languages that do not recognize color, cultures that do not distinguish numbers past the first multiple value, and gluttons who cannot tell an éclair from a profiterole. Culinary enthusiasts may be angered by the latter; the example before it is likely to give mathematicians a breather; but only a linguist could look at all three and argue for a strong case of linguistic relativism.

On to the resulting issue, confusions such as these should not under any circumstance deter us from the pursuit of meaning, or as I have noticed among many, cause us to abandon our conviction that there even is such a thing as meaning. If anything, they should only warn us against the fallacy that is the overreliance on empiricism. Because the saving grace of language is that for every misunderstanding that may arise out of a conflict in word meaning, one will find examples to the opposite; at whichever point in the cellular chain a misunderstanding may have arisen, there has been another within the same structure that has helped to clear it up, and has so inspired understanding out of disorder. If a pupil heard of a centurion with his crested helmet, gladius in hand, commanding his troops, though he may not be familiar with the meaning of the word centurion, the contextual cues will most likely trigger the correct category by means of intentional association. People of my generation did not know about centerfolds, but the context of the song was too clear not to understand the word. And if a man who knows nothing about trains were told to point at the cow-catcher of the locomotive, he could easily tell which part *that* is. You see, I do not deny that we stumble into confusion (I do not even deny the extent to which we do this), but it is only by being inheritors of understanding that we can recognize it, and it is by the fact of our recognition that we know we can also correct it. Because whenever we get lost, we know-not-how, in whichever blunder, we-know-not-where, the answer is always somewhere along the conceptual line.

Whenever we make a mistake in language, it is not language itself that is at fault, but our skill with it. So we had better optimize our technique, and ensure that both ends of the conceptual current are in order – that sense and reference are both sound. Without faith in our linguistic competence, we might as well surrender all of our competences to stupidity. Dismissing our only claim to understanding as inherently flawed, we will find ourselves forced to concede that misunderstanding, being inseparable from language, is as original as understanding, and that, by necessity, misunderstanding becomes not the antithesis of understanding, but its master – for if the two are not opposed to each other, with the positive at all times superior to the negative, the established equality out of their former contrast will reconfigure the positive as just an illusory subset of the negative. If having a penny and not having a penny were worth the same, that is, if you could buy nothing with either, then it is not the penniless person who is financially rich, but the stooge with the coin who is financially poor. One cannot argue for a total fallibility of argument without sacrificing the validity of his own argument. You may call it crazy, and I know it is crazy, because it is true – and *that* is all we are qualified to be.

And it really is a qualification – to the extent that it conveniently evokes this next domain of job applications. I am yet to see one that demands that the ideal candidate must have the kind of qualifications that are without deviation indispensable for the position. Though I have scoffed at applications taking the time to add that they are looking for an honest, sociable, hardworking person (as if anybody would be looking for a lazy sociopath that kicks puppies),[23] I am yet to encounter an application for, say, a news anchor, demanding that the ideal candidate must be able to speak, or an application for a delivery man that only accepts candidates with a functioning pair of legs. The truly essential quality is always assumed to be understood without it being explicitly stated. It is the same with language.

In every claim we make, we oblige ourselves to a set of truths just to enable the circumstances by which this one claim may be given the chance to be correct. If we said that Napoleon experienced his first defeat in battle at Leipzig, we are saying that there was such a man as Napoleon, that his business had to do with battles, that there was such a place as Leipzig, and that, until this specific battle in it, Napoleon was undefeated; we also oblige ourselves to the claim that this happened in the past by the tense we use, and the implication that there will be more losses for Napoleon in his future by not calling his first defeat his only defeat. Of course, a statement may omit many such entailments, which is what accounts for vagueness – an insufficiency of truths on which a truth-claim depends; redundancy, on the other hand, is a repeated commitment to the same truth, such as the expression "his first and only." I will quickly add that some apparent redundancy is not redundancy if the repetition is used for effect (do not forget the importance of context and the

---

[23] Though, to be fair, I have not looked at applications for lawyers or bankers.

quantum dolls). Above all other truths, however, no matter the argument, and regardless of its vagueness or redundancies, we oblige ourselves to the claim that what we say is true, and that, by extension, truth is knowable. Every declarative sentence begins with a presumed, inaudible: *it is true that*, or alternatively concludes with: *and that is true*. Seldom mentioned, this commitment to truth is the essential qualification for language: without it, you can merely squawk bark or screech – perchance to scream.

But unlike visible qualification, such as being able to speak or possessing a working pair of legs, invisible qualities can be faked. As a matter of fact, just about all of them have been faked already. We have all seen news anchors who, though able to speak, can only do so at a third-grade level; or delivery men who despite their legs may as well crawl to the right address. The illusion works best when the lack of an invisible quality is covered up with a visible representative: invisible education is faked with a diploma, invisible beauty is faked with makeup, invisible masculinity with muscle – you get the gist. Likewise, the invisible commitment to truth, which is the cornerstone of language, is faked, among those who lack it, with its most common representatives: signs and utterances, which, like diplomas and the semblance of beauty and muscles, tend to coincide with the real quality, but can nonetheless appear without it. Unfortunately for the deceiver, this tends to backfire. Masculinity is confronted, knowledge is tested, and makeup – well, you've seen them. And what happens next? There is gaslighting, shifting of blame, even more makeup, plastic surgery, threats of violence – the deceiver flings all the deception of which he is capable, hoping to maintain the illusion when threatened. The languageless person is no different. Having seen his dishonesty come to light, he will spin a web of confusion to blot out the truth. And this is how you notice dishonest policies and men: they rely the most on broken concepts; on vagueness and redundancies; on contradictions; on words with no meaning; on words which sense is more convenient than real. When you call them out, they just might retreat for a while – never for good, so do keep your guard up. But here is how you recognize the most dishonest of policies and men – the most competent (or at least the most ardent) of deceivers: they need you to be stupid. If you would rather be intelligent, they will try to convince others of your stupidity. Thought must be silenced, and minds must be deafened. A person in enmity with critical thinking will either feed you a lie because you are not qualified to think, or he will judge you an unqualified thinker for rejecting his lie.

And this is the great disqualifier. The marriage of dishonesty and stupidity. The replacement of language with prompt and reaction. Any time a person in (any kind of) power notices that a calculator does not know it is calculating, realizes that the gadget's ignorance of itself is no obstacle to it doing its job as he pushes the buttons, and concludes that it is the same with mankind: it does not matter what you think (or if you think) as long as you consent to having buttons installed on you. You are disqualified from his world the moment the thought crosses his mind. You are disqualified from the rest of the world the moment that same thought nests within yours.

Before you are tempted to agree with such a fate, in case you lack the good sense to reject it on principle, consider what kind of entity is the only entity other than yourself capable of pushing your buttons, and realize that the only creature we know to do this is just another man. So unless you yourself can be the master of your own intellect, the stewardship you will have rejected for laziness or pleasure or security (or whatever) will result not in an abandonment of the system – the fallibility of human ambition – but of a total submission to it. So, to the hedonistic reader: in your rejection of critical thinking, in your condescension to prompts, in your positing your commitment to truth as secondary to pleasure, you have not in fact become liberated from anxiety or error or what have you. You have not become wild and free. On the contrary. You have only become thoroughly domesticated.

<u>The Broken Echo</u>

It turns out that, following a tendon-injury, the exercises one must perform to get his body functioning as it used to are the antithesis of ego-lifting. After the prescribed break, a man eager to resume with his athletic hobby will find himself getting sore curling a 7kg dumbbell. Something similar can be said of all injuries: they take you back to beginner-level. A sprained ankle makes a painful challenge out of elementary dancing moves, and a broken knee means learning to walk all over again. This does not apply, however, to being simply *out of practice* in something. If you have not played the guitar in years, returning to the instrument might start you off rusty, and you may find you have lost your touch with hard solos, but the popular songs you were able to strum as a beginner, you will be able to strum as a returning adept right away. You will play and sing and your audience will enchantedly sing along if you care to imagine an audience. So now that I consider how conceptually lost we are, I realize the blow we must have taken at some indeterminate point before we forgot the meanings of basic words. Before we devolved from eloquent people into well-trained parrots. We are not merely *out of practice* with language. Rather, we have suffered an injury that has caused our conceptual tendons to grow back weaker. How and when, I know not.

Just today, I heard a proposition, made in a formal setting, and by a respected individual, meeting the agreement of many, that the fatal assault of medical personnel should be subject to harsher persecution than usual, as the loss of medical personnel is a major blow to medicine. Only a severe injury to one's intellectual faculties can lead one to posit the loss of life as a loss suffered by an institution as opposed to the individuals directly affected by it. Any argument that this is so because medical personnel take care of patients is nullified, seeing as the lives of these patients have been devalued in the proposition that, should one of the doctor's patients suffer a similar assault, the perpetrator should be persecuted to a lesser degree, seeing as his victim was *not even a doctor*. On another exemplary tangent, lately I have been hearing iterations of a conviction that has become so ingrained in the western mind, that it is more of a religious creed than an actual opinion. It is the belief that the modern rite of passage for young adults is renting cheap apartments and working menial jobs. Apparently, young people become *independent* and *start lives of their own* by giving their lives to their employers so they may remain dependent on their landlords. It cannot be but a serious intellectual sprain that has made it difficult for us to even understand such simple concepts as *human life* and *independence*.

Perhaps the injury was a tendon that, not allowed to develop, grew weaker instead of stronger with each session. It had too much fatigue and not enough recovery. This is how you develop tendinopathy in the literal world by the way. All the same, by the tested method of healing an injury, if we are to recover our conceptual competencies, we must start light – small concepts, simple meanings, easy questions. We will build up to the load that justifies the hard rock playlist as we get stronger.

It was during one such exercise session that the song "Fortuneteller" by Deep Purple came up in my playlist. I found the lyrics easy to relate to. It got to a part where the speaker sings "Some days come with a vengeance / Some days I feel – " I did not get the next phrase. Perhaps it was *I feel the pain*, with which I can relate, or perhaps it was *I feel so frail*, to which I can also relate. It might have been a poetic phrase, such as *I feel so pale*, which, though not a feeling, I can at least imagine what it must *feel like* to feel pale, and that too is relatable. He might have said *I feel so vague*, and, guess what: I also feel so... vaguely vague sometimes. This is because, for every concept that describes us, we are also the referential entity that verifies the concept; so when part of a concept is accepted as applicable, the rest of it is likely to be assumed as accurate. Even if we mishear the next line, we will interpret it as complementary to the part we like. I doubt I would have considered the latter relatable if I had disagreed with the former. Consider that relatively modern song that is about being happy – you know the one, the singer is happy and happiness is somewhere, either in the room, or the womb, on the moon, or it goes vroom (whatever), he repeats it over and over, and its lyrics I consider not even remotely relevant to my situation – even when I do feel happy. Do you notice anything strange in that? Something alluding to total subjectivity but also a law applying universally to concept and conceptualization? It is the peculiarity that, though I can imagine feeling pale, which is a rather weird expression, a much simpler metaphor, such as happiness being in the room, is to me as senseless as happiness going vroom.

For the record, I am not depressed; I merely dislike music that (to my ears) sounds a pitch bend away from a kitten doing jumping jacks. Art should not seek to appeal to short-term suggestibility; whatever emotion it causes in its audience must be a secondary effect, not the original intention. With that said, let us keep in mind that conceptualization is not exclusively of the rational mind. There are degrees of emotion, of will, and of personal disposition that play into our ability to form concepts, to analyze concepts, and to evaluate truth – the reality we perceive is the reality we conceive. It depends on more than mind and object. I think how I feel, and I feel what I experience. Nobody is above this – especially not those who have deluded themselves with the pride that they are immune to it (the irony that their pride accounts for this very bias proves it perfectly).

Now, consider the injury we have sustained: we cannot carry much weight conceptually. Next, remember the chapter "The Silent Indoctrinator" (10), and how indoctrination can function without language, i.e. it can rely solely on undefined feelings. Lastly, imagine mankind, feeling *so vague*, unable to make sense of it, and susceptible to whatever concept a manipulative ruler may scribble onto our pale anxieties. Propaganda is obsolete. The modern tools of indoctrination are significantly more potent.

I think I know what happened. Given the non-reasonable arbiters of inference (I do not call them unreasonable, let alone wrong; only that they are not part of reason), which we could group as sentiment (as in emotion and experience), and seeing as inference echoes conviction, regarding which sentiment, though capable of informing us, second-handedly, of an external truth, is itself not concerned with external truth as much subjective experience, it becomes necessary to expand the unspoken entailments of propositions with another essential handle: just as a proposition is followed by *and that is true* or is preceded by *it is true that*, propositions are also forwarded by *it is my conviction that* or concluded with *and that is my conviction*, respectively. This matters because whereas one handle claims objectivity, the other is a subjective disclaimer. We could splice the two into *The world in which I live is such that* or *that is my account* as a conclusion, with an emphasis on the personal pronoun. And if you have been following my argument carefully, you might have foreseen my next point: it is the subjective half that we trust the most, especially in lieu of knowledge (which we almost always lack) – from the historical enthusiast disregarding the suffering of the enemy, to the chauvinist calling the Natives uncivilized, to the same historical enthusiast feeling pale because happiness goes vroom, the more prominent half of our mental experiences is a self-centered affair. Keeping in mind that what we experience of reality is akin to an echo, somewhat clear and somewhat muddled, the conceptual chain its transposition into sensible words, does it not follow that an echo in my world will likely sound like an echo that happens to belong in this world of mine? What each of us believes is not necessarily a reflection of a state of affairs, but a reflection of ourselves: of who we are and what we think and what applies to us the best. This is not a condoning of the genetic fallacy. On the contrary, it is an explanation of why people are susceptible to fallacies. It is no use informing a cultist of the contradictions in his belief – of his misunderstanding of things he does not know, when he did not become convinced by the things he did *not* hear, but the things that he did hear: the things he knows, the echo he understood, the part that fits him, his world, and his witness. So how terrible our collective injury, that the echo we hear now is of an inhuman world, as we are herded towards subhuman interpretations?

But that is no cause for despair. Yes, we are lost, and yes, the concepts we need are too confusing for us as we are – ineloquent, unread, too tired to read effectively, and frankly not paid enough to take up the challenge. But though we are weak, we will get stronger if we know where to start. We will start with concepts that have been mapped for us already. We will work to a common meaning from what we know: from what we hear, on to what we can make out. We begin with "Some days come with a vengeance," and go from there. We may mishear the next line, but we do not mishear the lines that come after. Soon, the vagueness is filled with lyrics that describe it: regret, a rash decision, loneliness, desperation, reflection... what we now tend to trivialize as depression, and believe scammers when they dub it *a lack of dopamine*, becomes a set of things we can at last identify: things in the outside world and things within us, things we can change and things we wish to see changed. Just so, conceptualization can be likened to the attempt to figure out the lyrics to a song which lyrics we do not know. What we call theory is really just the presumption of completed stanzas – sometimes accurate, and often taught in schools irrespective of their accuracy. Academic dispute is, ideally, a debate on whether it says "Some days I feel so bad" or "Some days I feel so bale."

The next chapter deals with the way metaphor plays into the scheme. Yes, we are back at metaphor. This section began as an argument to prove its value. To show that metaphorical meaning is valid – just as valid as what we call literal meaning, which is really no more than conventionalized meaning, and the kind of meaning that, you will soon see why, offers only half of the sense present in indirect meaning: behind the unspoken mapping of reality, there is, primarily, the eloquent fullness of metaphor and its kin.

<u>The Quiet Cartographer</u>

And so, we have established the workings of the semantic process. We have, moreover, argued for the necessity of the semantic process. If a man is to call himself the master of his own volition, or at least free from the will of another man, he must be willing to run the conceptual legacy of his choice through his own conceptual filter. In order to ensure that lunacy has not usurped his stewardship, he must also keep in mind the performance of his conceptual filter in reference to a standardized system of understanding. This is important to note as my argument is not that a man must reject all conceptual suggestion – only that he must consider its meaning. In so doing, he does not only guarantee his own conceptual freedom, but also his part in humanity. Humanity, if one must visualize man as a machine, is really a machinery for learning. We take in phenomena and we generate knowledge; for all we know, being the only species capable of this, and lagging far behind other species in terms of propagation of the specie, physical feats, or the capacity for pleasure in pleasure bereft of knowledge, our uniqueness obliges us to generate knowledge in the same way that the uniqueness of the guitar obliges the guitarist not to use it as a coaster. The conceptual process is an essential part of this, since it exists to assign meaning and to refine it. It maps out what we consider knowledge. It creates borders, and it expands and contracts them where necessary.

Nowhere is this as evident as it is in metaphor. Metaphor, we know, is the rendering of a subject A through the means commonly employed to communicate subject B. With that, if we try to present metaphor on the conceptual chain, the semantic tissue, it would look like so.

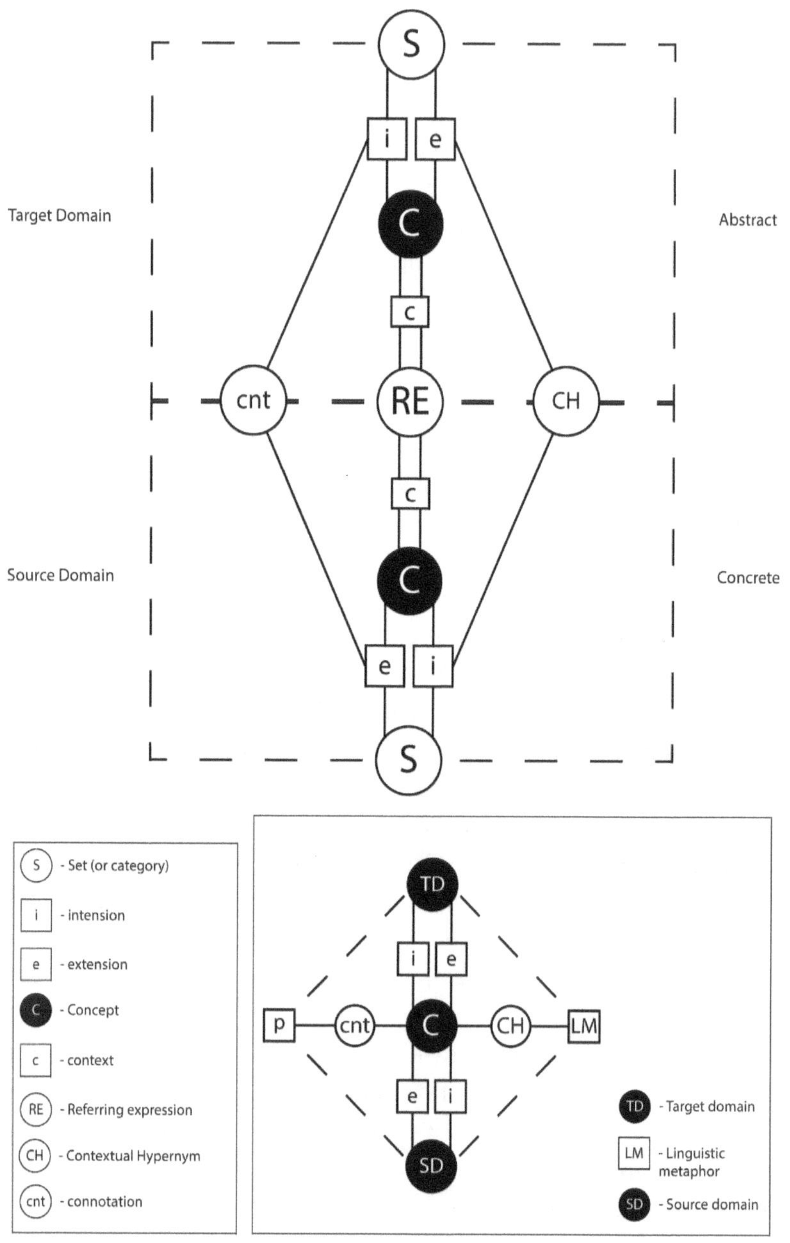

Fig. 3: Metaphor on the conceptual chain.

The source domain is the reference of the target domain. A textbook conceptual metaphor is the metaphor AN ARGUMENT IS WAR. In fig. 3, you can fill in the interaction between the domains. We begin with a perceived dispute; let this be the set, which we conceptualize with an intention containing such senses as disagreement, a degree of hostility, and conflict, then allow it to cover any behavior considered a dispute as its extension, and direct it to the concept that, not of a singular meaning, is the conceptual metaphor ARGUMENT IS WAR. War, in turn, being the reference, is contextualized to a concept we have determined with the intension of conflict, hostility, attacking, defending, winners, losers, negotiations, armament, casualties, reparations... In forming a reference from these collections of meanings, we contextually select only those elements that are compatible with the senses of the target domain. This way, the concept of argument comes in contact only with those elements of war that are compatible with argument: conflict, attacking, defending, winning, losing (and such), but not armament, military technology, military ranks (and such). The construct so created is what I refer to as a hypothetical contextual hypernym. Like a hypernym, it contains many subsets called hyponyms, but, unlike a proper hypernym, it is entirely dependent on the context – it exists only as long as we select those specific senses of the source intension that can cover the extension of the target. This is why we can speak of advancing a thesis or defending an argument or attacking a proposition.

If we invert the process,[24] i.e. we call forth attributes from the intension of what has so far been the target domain, in our case ARGUMENT, and conform them to the extension of WAR, you will find that the connotation of war changes accordingly: expressions used to describe argument become expressions that

---

[24] Look at the left side of the conceptual chain;

describe war – we say things like *The United States slapped Nazi Germany in the face*, or *The Finnish army made a mockery of the Soviet invasion* or *The Rebels agreed to the terms of the North*; we speak of *blundering retreats* and *convincing victories*...

When we say that the purpose of metaphor is to explain one object in terms of another, we really mean to say that whatever we observe in the world but cannot determine with certainty, or whatever echo we hear but cannot be too sure it says what we think it says, becomes subjected to the explanatory scope of what we can confidently say we have determined of something else – an echo we have previously deciphered, and in this context appears to sound a lot like the echo we are hearing at present. Metaphor exists to map new knowledge based on knowledge in which we are already confident. This is what allows for the partial interchangeability between domains: how, at one point, a person calling out the flaws in the argument of another is said to be attacking their argument, since argument is war, and how, at another point, the winning side in a given war is said to have accomplished a convincing victory, since war can be an argument. The applicability of one domain to another can vary, and so does their frequency of use; in general, it is one dynamic that has been conventionalized, and its reversal that is being used poetically or ad-hoc.

This all depends on the contextual hypernym: a non-word that contains the determined determining meaning of one phenomenon and the referential scope of the phenomenon which undetermined determining meaning is being established. The contextual hypernym is not something one hears, but it is something one understands whenever they get the metaphor. It is the border of sense, and a mapper of meaning. It stands between what we know and what we seek to understand. It is not spoken, but it is always consulted. To many, it is negligible, but all would be lost without it. It is a conceptual landmark; in essence the North Star, and in practice the library of Alexandria. It is the quiet cartographer.

Frère Jacques

This is what I call to attention when I argue for the universal sense of brotherhood. It is the contextual hypernym that determines the conditions under which the category of *shared experience* can be directed to the referential representative of *brother*. Look at the scheme and consider the interaction. There is the intention of shared existence, and there is the extension of everyone you know. The reference is, of course, *brother* (the reference being the source domain). We *extend* the extension to anyone you could expect to hear referred to by that name, be it your biological brother, your brothers at church, or your brother bikers. The intension, we determine by... well, how does one relate to a brother? You grow up together, you share genetic code, you share property such that each is entitled to his own share; you also fight, though you are not supposed to, and you might not care much for each other, though this is described as *unbrotherly*.

On the one hand, there is perfect compatibility between the source intension and the target extension: being human, we all have similar genes; we all have some property (entitled to a piece, but not to the whole); we grow up under similar circumstances... you get the picture. And we also fight, though we are not supposed to, and we do not appear to care much for one another, and that too is described as unbrotherly. So is it not strange then that just as the two domains are compatible, in neutral and hostile contexts, the contextual hypernym rejects this compatibility? For though the intension of *brother* and the extension of *everybody you know* can meet under circumstances of fighting and bullying and dislike, still, the metaphor that is *brother* suggests a moral obligation that codes the opposite of such senses, owing to which the word *brotherly* means what it does. So we need to explain the specific selection (or elimination) of certain semantic constituents of the intension of brother: the reason it is exclusively moral behavior that is compatible with the contextual hypernym.

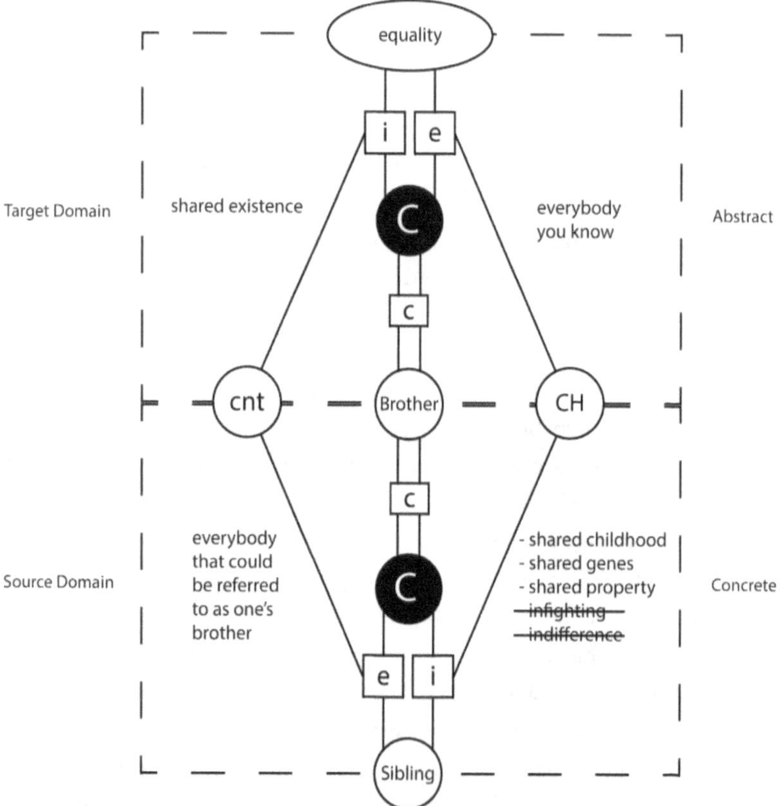

Fig. 4: The metaphor of brotherhood.

I will here ask you to remember the opposite process. When what is assumed to be the target domain comes to extend its intension to the extension of the source domain – the relative interchangeability between domains, by which the initial source domain becomes conceptually altered by its former target domain. On one end, we have all the people we may call *brother*. This pairs on the other end with the sense of shared existence, which, since sharing entails an equal right to what is being shared, we will designate as the category of *equality*. And as the treatment of one condones the same treatment to all who are equal to *one*, the just treatment of others is a moral obligation we have to our equals, in as far as it is how we expect to be treated ourselves. Do you now begin to see the true interaction between the domains? At last, they have become compatible with the moral demand of the hypernym. It is quite the spin.[25]

For it is not biological brotherhood that gives us the idea of *true brotherhood*, which we then go on to romanticize into love and care and respect for our fellow man. It is the other way around. It is that we recognize ourselves and we recognize our fellow man; we recognize we have an equal right to existence, and the love we expect is the love we understand we are expected to give. And so we hear the echo, we sail conceptual waters, and we consider the sound; we look to the North Star, and we let the quiet cartographer guide us. We see our (literal) siblings, so like us, so equal to ourselves that we share even the same genes and the same parents and the same slice of life; and the cartographer maps this new category: equality perfected. Conceptually, the expected harmony between man and man is not an ideological extrapolation of biological brotherhood; biological brotherhood is a hyponym of the expected harmony between man and man.

---

[25] Some might disagree that sharing entails equality. *I can have 80% of the share and another merely 20% of it, and that is still sharing!* they might argue. But it is not so. For I bring up the right to an equal share, not the obligation to share the same amount. The dynamic is, after all, a subject of consent, not numbers. If we shared a car, and I worked from home, you can have 95% of the car at your convenience. But if I happen to need it, and you do not let me use it, even a 50-50 deal will become skewed into usurpation. You are entirely entitled to what is yours, as am I to mine – but a common good, our right to dignity included, must be equally accessible to all; otherwise, it will be neither common nor good, but an usurped resource, itself in need of liberation.

<h1 style="text-align:center"><u>Disputable Implications</u></h1>

Do not mistake me for an optimist by the way. I am sure there are people who do not expect any love from me, and so for the reason that they do not care to offer me any in return. The only kind of brotherhood they understand is the kind marked by sibling rivalry and property disputes. They deem themselves deserving of a bigger share – not of what they own, but of what I own. They would not have me as a brother, but as a slave; a feudal peasant at best. They do not consider me their equal. They do not consider you their equal either. I am conceptually obliged to see them as my brothers regardless. And so are you. Else, we could not condemn their unbrotherly behavior, but will have to congratulate them for it instead – after all, there is nothing wrong in not being brotherly to a man who is not your brother.

Having said that, I admit, though I talk big, I do not feel the adequate sentiment. How can a person who hates me possibly be my brother? The cartographer nods. He has mapped the phenomenon already. There is a word for everything, including the kind of brother who hates his brothers. *Cain* comes to mind. *Traitor* is another. *Stupid* fits them best. Like rabid animals, they are to be kept at a distance, and, like rabid animals, they are to be pitied. For they are not themselves malice incarnate. They are rather *misunderstanding incarnate* – a progressively fleshier incarnation of an ever expanding stupidity. They fail to recognize their brothers, they fail to understand what it means to be brotherly, and they fail to even consider the possibility that there might be something worth learning. Yes, I am the type to draw a demon as a blubbering idiot. So no, I do not think they are capable of thinking. Sure, they can plot and they can calculate, but that is not thinking. Calculation is no more a sign of thinking than a calculator is a sign of sentient life.

To put it bluntly, I am not telling anybody to treat his aggressor as his brother. I am merely suggesting that if the aggressor-to-be understood that his victims are his brothers, he would have cancelled the carrying out of his ill intent before those people became his victims. But if he still chose to act unbrotherly, his power to do so could not overpower the multitudes if they saw themselves for the family they are. If you do not believe me, consider how the imminence of disaster in modern projections is always a weakness of separation – a crisis we could easily survive if not for social apathy: there would be no population decline if not for the pandemic of loneliness; there would be no loneliness if not for the alienation of the individual; there would be no alienation if an alienating society were worth upholding. The economy could be fixed in a moment if everybody understood, at the same time, that they ought not to steal from their brothers, and that their brothers ought not to be left to starve. Neither hell nor high taxes can threaten a loving family.

And still, there are those among you who do not believe me. The aggressor, however – he does believe me. In fact, he has possibly known this long before I discovered it, and, in case anybody comes by it, he has made sure to counter reality by obstructing its acceptance. The ideological templates at our disposal, though mortally opposed to one another, are obliged to notions that, even if by contrary means, find common ground in that they are opposed to the argument I bring up here. On one end of the political spectrum there are people who recoil at the mere mentioning of equality – *Gah! It's collectivist propaganda!* even though I am not a collectivist; and, on the other end, people will recoil at the notion of brotherhood – *Bleugh! It's Puritan!* even though I am not a puritan either. This is not the work of the cartographer. There is nothing wrong in either equality or brotherhood. The confusion is clearly a prompt or a reaction to one. Whether the aggressor that makes these particular prompts is an individual person, a collective, an idea, some supernatural principality, or man's irrational appeal for self-destruction, I am not in the position to say.

It is all the more ironic that my argument is in danger of being rejected on political grounds. I do not write any of this intending to compose a political treatise. My essay is a mere conceptual guide. I hold concept to be above politics. It is impossible to give a measured analysis from a slanted perspective. How could we make just laws if we cannot define justice, and how could we define justice if we do not even care what that word means? The question of humanity comes before the question of governing humanity. The question of brotherhood is pivotal to any debate. You cannot help your nation if you have already failed your family – that is, your brothers. I do not suppose you count on the prime minister to fix your family squabbles. It is ever the latter that this section aims to address. The answer to family dispute is not a political reform; the answer to family dispute is to say, *Brother, I do not think you have been treating me the way you should want me to treat you in return.*

Without that proposition, no system will ever be just. And though some people are less brotherly than others, we all own an equal share of reality. There is no other purpose to dispute than to remind ourselves of this. There cannot be brotherhood without equality, and there will never be equality without a universal acknowledgment of brotherhood. The two are one and the same. And if you have picked up on the pattern I began with the title of this chapter, brotherhood and equality are also one and the same with liberty.

The Wings of Liberty

Yes, this was an essay on liberty all along. Didn't Locke's discussions also steer that way? So why should their complement, admittedly but one of many and overdue by a few centuries, not do the same? Any restraint on conceptual movement is an assault against liberty. This is best seen exactly in the semantic butchering of that word – liberty, which has been so abused by poor definitions and by the gradual replacement of definitions with prompts, that I am only glad for the metaphor that will help bring it to light: what it means, and which part of its sense we must retrieve.

The conceptual metaphor in question is FREEDOM IS A BIRD. It is a productive metaphor with many derivatives, including the simile *free as a bird* and the symbol of the eagle as a representative of freedom. The intuitive antonym of liberty is slavery, but, not being (lexically) a binary category, it has taxonomic pairs in busyness and obligation – consider, *I am not free tonight, for I am busy with work*, or *I am not free, I must take care of the baby*. Betimes, the opposite of freedom is justice, if the word is spoken in the context of a just judicial system. Now, it would be weird to say that freedom really is a great thing, such as when you are not a slave, but also when justice has been cheated, and when you are unemployed and have nobody to care for. Conversely, we cannot say that freedom is good only *some* of the time, but often (arguably most of the time) freedom is patently bad. Freedom must always be good, and slavery and the negligence of duty must always be bad. So where do we go from there? It seems that we have heard an echo, and it seems that we hear it in more ways than we can make sense of whatever it has been trying to say. Let us consult the cartographer.

The extension of whatever we consider a representative of the concept of freedom must be compatible with a set of intentional senses that form our understanding of the concept of bird. The obvious one is, of course, flight. From our perspective, the bird's freedom is so thorough that it is not constrained even by gravity. But this is not the full picture. Because we have not so far, by the virtue of disregarding gravity, thought to explain freedom as an airplane, a random object in space, or a bat. The thing that makes avian flight distinct in the context is the conjunction of will and directedness together with flight. An airplane does fly, but it is controlled by the will of another, namely the pilot; an object in space is devoid of direction as it floats aimlessly; and the flight of the bat is so erratic to observe, so inelegantly chaotic, that it does not metaphorize as something soaring through the bright skies, but is instead conceptualized in an expression of disorder (which, I assume, if I mention now, might be one reference too many). So yes, liberty is a bird because liberty is not constrained by anything – not even by gravity – but also because liberty is of oneself, as is the will of the bird, it is directed toward a goal, as is a bird's gliding through the air, and it is clear to see, unhidden and uninhibited, just as birds fly during the day. Such is the conceptualization of freedom when it is likened to a bird. Going by the contextual hypernym, the meaning of freedom is, indeed, a lack of chains, or an ownership of one's will without the intermission of a foreign will, but only as long as this lack of chains has been put to good use. Otherwise, you are just a bat out of hell. There: I said it.

The opposite process is just as interesting. When we consider the interaction between the extension of bird and the intension of freedom, the extension of bird being the set of creatures we recognize by the word, what we notice is that the intention of freedom does not consistently cover all birds. The bald eagle is almost synonymous with freedom. The barnyard hen is never mistaken for it. The captivity of the latter is a major reason for its lack of metaphorization. However, let us not forget the initial sense that qualifies avian species as free. It is the same sense by which a penguin or an emu does not fit the category either, though they do not live in captivity. This is, of course, the fact of flight. Only flying birds get to be free – none of that phoned-in chicken double-jump or the sophistic *underwater flight* of the penguin. If a bird is to fit the metaphor, it must be completely capable of flight and willing to engage in it. And so, we know that liberty must also be absolute: it must be total, and it must not be threatened by if-clauses.

If a man is free in one regard, and *grounded* in another, he is no freer than a barnyard hen. Do note, a barnyard hen is not a likelier metaphor for liberty than an emu on account that it can fly *just a bit higher*. In this case, flight is not a scalar category. And neither is freedom. You either have it in total, or you only have it on paper. And it must be so with all men if we are to ever call ourselves free. Because as long as some men have more freedoms than others, what we call freedom will continue to resemble a relative category. If some men are freer than others, then men will know their freedoms by contrast. And, while you may perceive enough personal liberties to liken yourself to an eagle, under such a system, we have no way of knowing if we are not just a breed of chickens that can fly just a little higher than some of their mates. The disillusion will become tangible as soon as a bird of prey chances to swoop down upon us, and we realize that we too have lived as clucking slaves. Even if you are convinced, without any possibility for doubt, of your own personal freedom, the possibility for comparison between the liberties you experience and the slavery of others frames your existence not as living in freedom, but as living outside slavery. As long as there exist circumstances by which you recognize your brothers as slaves, you will remain a slave to whatever is stopping you from granting the enslaved their freedom.

In more mundane, practical terms, if there are men who do not answer to the law to which you answer, or if you are forced into an occupation that is not your calling, or if you are unable to find your place in the world for a fluke of history, as long as any random factor threatens your equals with the same probabilities, the world you inhabit is not a shared existence or a liberated civilization, but a scalar system of tyranny, servitude, and sibling rivalries. I assure you, you do not want a Big Brother.

But what do you mean freedom must not be limited? I can imagine some asking. *You must put some constraints on freedom, else it is anarchy! You can't have people breaking the law and stealing and such, can you?* Some people think that unbridled freedom is a gateway to chaos. But I did not say we should do away with laws. Laws, if they are just, do not serve to limit freedom – on the contrary, they exist to guarantee freedom; for example, the criminalization of theft protects my freedom to own what I have earned – just as the lack of legislature against exploitation limits my financial freedom to earn what I have worked for. Laws are not the enemy. The careful reader knows this already. We have talked about direction and about flying in daylight. When we are free, we will fly in harmony – no, not all of us in the same direction, of course: some will fly south, some will be returning north, others will be making nests... but the important thing is that none will be a nuisance to the other; freedom can be the bald eagle, the peaceful dove, or the carefree sparrow, but not the predatory eagle or the thieving crow. I did not say we have no (moral) bonds; I said we have no chains – which includes those faux liberties that, tethering their slaves to wild whim, account for the rabid contortions of the bat – in hell or out of it.

And what of the criminal then? Or the person who says he is not free because he is working, or the person who looks for a babysitter so he may be free? What of them? Those are simply cases of concept short-circuiting. They do not fit the metaphor because they stem from a mistaken conceptual frame. I would argue it is an error of reference, to say that a convicted felon has been set *free*, while he remains a slave to his guilt (or if he cannot feel guilt, a slave to his mental sickness), not to mention a threat to the freedom of others. Similarly, to mistake being free to go clubbing with liberty is an error of category, in that people who say this do not usually think that word even has a meaning, but instead use it to conveniently describe a preferable set of external circumstances.

And the bald eagle? That bird is also a symbol of liberty, but it is a thieving carnivore! Is the predator also part of your avian utopia? Not necessarily. In as far as Benjamin Franklin complained that "For my own part I wish the bald eagle had not been chosen as the representative of our country. He is a bird of bad moral character. He does not get his living honestly" (1784), the bird of prey might have been a referent chosen too hastily. But I believe the better explanation here is that the bald eagle has been chosen as a symbol of liberty not for the quality of being a predator, but for the quality of not being anybody's food; that is what makes him free, his diet notwithstanding. The fact that it looks cool might have also played a part in the metaphorization. Thankfully, the consequence of this minor confusion has not been an aggressive mindset on the part of people associated with the symbol: their interpretation of liberty has not been altered into a predatory mentality. If it were (hypothetically, of course), then that would only further attest for what I have been saying – mistaken concepts lead to ruin.

Still, this is only if we try to expand your metaphor, some might argue, in their enduring obstinacy. Only if we assume that a brother must be somebody with whom you grow up and share things, or if we assume that the flight of a bird is directed and whatnot... but if we just said 'a brother is a male sibling' and 'a bird is free because it flies' your argument means nothing! You have based all that you have said on overthinking simple expressions. But it is not so.

I have come to measure the moral pretentiousness of a secular text by how long it takes before it quotes from the Bible. I assume I have put enough text between the beginning and this point that I should be cleared of moralist charges. So to the reader who clings to the belief that I have corrupted the meaning of brother and the metaphor of bird with their extended intensions, I will just give this one final piece of advice: get yourself access to the Old Testament (preferably the *New International Version*), and look up Leviticus 11.13-19.

The Conquest of Concept

The Controversial Essay

Welcome back. We have completed the technical section. If you have skipped it, either on account of its technicality or my suggestion, then the arguments ahead should be no less clear for the fact, as I am true to my word. Mostly.[26]

I will begin this chapter with some controversy. Not because what I write next is the part where I finally reveal my secret political agenda, but because I will say something that tends to put most people on edge: I will say a word or few on theology. No, I am not trying to recruit you into a cult. I can only guess why theology has gotten that stigma – the suspicion that whoever talks about the subject is by necessity a proselytizer. Why, if somebody begins discussing sexual theory, do you instantly assume they are trying to seduce you? In a nightclub, maybe – but in a nightclub, it is the setting that determines intent, not the conversation. I will talk about theology for the purpose of illustrating the power of concept. And what better example of total conceptual devotion than a kind of philosophy that is theory as well as practice, and which claims to know not the world, but what lies beyond it – an intellectual system bordering the closest with intangible$_2$ as even our minds cannot know the ways of its subject (John 3.8, Isaiah 55.8-9); the only glimmer of tangibility$_2$ allowed is the degree of tangibility we have been willed capable of recognizing.

Christianity is a religion of concept. Yes, I chose the controversial religion. The one which adherents will tell you about the Gospel, which means *the good news*, in particular, the good news that everybody you know and love will (in all likelihood, together with the overwhelming majority of

---

[26] If there is any part that relies on an argument from the previous section, I will note the page or the chapter that contains it.

mankind) suffer unending torture for all eternity, though you may acquire bliss provided you can be indifferent to their suffering (for all eternity); then tell you that the Bible makes no financial suggestions with Matt. 19.21 or 1 Tim. 6.17-19, but read trickle-down economics in 2 Thess. 3.10. I assume I have made enough fun of Christians to be given the benefit of the doubt by my non-Christian readers. But believe it or not, there is an intellectual tradition in Christianity. And don't worry, I will not go into any of it here. I will instead try my hand at a personal contribution to that intellectual tradition. And it is in the sense that you read above: Christianity is a religion of concept.

It really does not offer anything else. Its theology is not a set of practices or of esoteric answers, but of conceptual nudges. It will not tell you anything about the shape of the Earth or wherever gods dwell; it has no secret knowledge to share but that which you are supposed to know already (Luke 17.21, Romans 2.14-17, Heb. 10.16-18). Christianity does not bless you to prosper, it does not promise rewards for doing well, and it does not offer to help you out of a jam. If you suffer, Christianity tells you that this is not what was meant for you; if you sin, it tells you this is not what you were meant to do; and, if you are virtuous, it tells you this is who you are meant to be. It is all concept, and nothing tangible₁. Christians might protest and say that it does offer something very important apart from concept, which is the salvation of one's soul, but, at the risk of sounding condescending, I believe that might be a bit off the mark: it is not Christianity that offers salvation, but God. I strongly doubt anyone would have any chance of being saved if God did not will to save them, and, as far as I understand Scripture, admittedly as an amateur, God does not will that anyone should be damned (2 Peter 3.9). To mistake a religion as the thing that saves a person is to fall for the same idolatry against which the Bible warns its readers. And do note that if idolatry is the perception of divinity within an object, then idolatry is really just a perversion of concept: a misunderstood intension of an object to include divinity, or a wrongful extension of divinity onto an object. From there, I would argue, theology that aspires to correct this error (by doing away with law and custom, by rejecting sacrifice and appeasement, by outright banning idol-worship) is a system devoted almost entirely to concept.

I am sure you have encountered the cliché of conflicted identity, in real life and culture alike: people not knowing who they *really* are, holding themselves to be secretly evil or uncaring or plot-bendingly perverted, of people changing as a result of something, and changing to such an extent that they are now lost in just how dramatically tough they have become, heroes at one moment, villains the next, redeemed just in time to get the girl – you get the picture. It was perhaps not a cliché at first. It might have been a question people were asking themselves long before movies were there to tell them they ought to ask it.[27] The most interesting example of this, which I call interesting for being so obvious yet (to my knowledge) not commonly considered, I have noticed in the New Testament, specifically, in the motif of mistaken identity juxtaposed to (let us call it) corrected identity. The beginning of The Gospel of John is quick to correct people that "this was not the Logos" (1.8) in regards to John the Baptist, and the latter is quick to correct people that he is not Elijah (1.20-21). The Gospel of Matthew begins with a genealogy to prove that the protagonist really is who the narrator says He is. Further into the story, there is a correction on the use of the word *brothers*, in particular, its extension (12.49). It is this same Word of Words who walks up to a woman referred to only as a "woman caught in adultery" (John 8.11) and tells her to "sin no more," which implies that this adulteress, a person whose identity in the story hinges on her practicing of this sin, ought to no longer practice the sin, and therefore lose the only designation by which she is presently recognized – whatever she becomes next, she cannot remain the word that she was. By the time

---

[27] If you have not yet chosen a subject for your thesis, you're welcome.

fishermen become "fishers of men" (Matt. 4.19) the alteration of identity should obtain the right to a motif. And as Peter, that was called Simon, acquires his new name and profession, he also experiences a change in personality from a rather cowardly person to a self-sacrificially courageous person – once called the "slanderer" (Mark 8.33), that was called Satan, he is presently called a saint. I have not gotten very far in the New Testament (or the Old Testament, for that matter), but I was made aware that the *Book of Revelation* (the cool one) depicts the redemption of creation in a scene where men walk up to their Creator to receive a white pebble on which they read their true names (MacDonald, "The New Name").

We crave to know who we are. We perceive all kinds of facts about ourselves, and, not immune to fictions on the subject, on our good days we dare to speculate, as on our bad days we boldly conclude. We write our personal histories, at once glorious, grueling, and disgusting. We have some idea of who we are. We have a good idea that these theories are not to be trusted. And in comes a Man, presumably of divine heritage, and He tells you He knows exactly who you are: not a fisherman, but a fisher of men; not a coward, but a courageous soldier in need of armor; not a Simon[28], but a Peter. Christianity begins as a subversion of concept. It is about assigning new intension for who you are and new extension for the things that you do. It is a change of referents from impotent mammals to the children of God. *But that is not who I am!* you might protest to the Holy Man. *I am a scoundrel, a fishmonger (the Shakespearean kind), I would betray my lord to save my skin, at my most heroic, I merely pretend!* Others may claim the opposite, *I am a paragon of virtue, I am unrepentantly bold, I am too good for mortal anxieties!* but to both camps, the response is "Depart from me, I never knew you" (Matt. 7.23), for He never knew such things – such poorly arranged categories and for such

---

[28] No offense meant to people named Simon; except for that one Simon I know, but I don't think he'd be reading this.

mistaken referents; omniscience does not recognize nonsense. And so it will remain until you assent to the new concept – to the concept that, the Holy Man tells you, is your true concept; He knows because it was Him that wrote it, and what better writer than a Man who, not merely a master of words, is said to be the Word itself.

I do not mean, of course, that Christian belief is a paradigm of cognitive linguistics. There is a lot more to it: ancient history, actual theology, medieval philosophy, dogma, custom, culture... Biblical hermeneutics do not stop at the purposes of my essay. Even the part I cited just above, I took from an excerpt that condemns boisterous religious people for their lack of love – not an encouraging pep-talk, which is how I might have inadvertently presented it. Still, if the sanctimonious "worker of iniquity" is somebody who does not love, then he remains a somebody who has got the wrong concept of God, a conceptual fluke directly addressed elsewhere (1 Corinth. 13.1-3, 1 John 4.7-8...19-21). So I never actually misrepresented or misinterpreted the verse. I merely shortened it to make it concise.[29]

This pattern of conceptual alteration can be seen in the social reform introduced by Christianity as well. The intensions of blessedness, wealth, and righteousness were all changed to exclude property and reputation, and to incorporate modesty and meekness in the place of worldly praise. The extension of each shifted from the privileged to the underprivileged. Self-improvement came to mean self-denial. The concept of savior changed from an ethnic military liberator to a peaceful universal

---

[29] Nowhere in the text is it implied that impious workers of iniquity will get a different answer. The verse does not condemn pious people as particularly sinful and therefore deserving of banishment; it rather argues that pious people lacking love are equally as astray as irreligious loveless people. The two are related by the concept of iniquity, which I here interpret (admittedly, possibly mistakenly) as the result of spiritual misconception. Neither can approach Omniscience while living in error, this error being spiritual stupidity.

liberator, while the concept of liberation shed the notion of political freedom and became an entirely new kind of freedom, such that those convinced of it the most were also the most fearless when facing political tyranny. Had the concept of liberty not changed, the people proclaiming the news of their liberator would have been a pitifully confused bunch, believing they had been freed while hiding from the authorities, and cowering from the sword as they professed immortality. The conceptual paradigm shifted in every respect that religion has ever been known to address: from the identity of man, to the identity of God, to concepts concerning virtue and salvation and religiosity. The restoration of the world began as a restoration of words.

This is true of any and all philosophical movements. Any ideology with the ambition to change the world has targeted the conceptual matrices of its followers – the success of every such ambition has relied on this step for its intellectual security. It is why I think discussions on economy are futile whenever they neglect language. They keep flaunting statistics to make their case, but the dispute is, in its origin, a conceptual debate: capitalism has worked to change the concept of labor; Marxism has tried to change the concept of history; Stalinism has made sure to change the concept of Marxism. Disputes between nations are often disputes on what constitutes a nation, or what concepts determine a nation's right to exist. And just about every social dispute stems from however the disputing sides understand the concept of humanity: what is man, what does he do, and how does he relate to his fellow men? Statistics regarding profit and social mobility and natality are meaningless unless at least two sides can agree on what they actually mean (or if they matter at all to the discussion).

But I really flatter the process. It isn't always an intellectual clash. It has been known to take place in entirely nonintellectual paradigms. Ideology is merely a vehicle for it, whenever it chances to opt for classier means of transport. A lot of the time, mass conceptual change begins as general confusion among the masses irrespective of belief. This happens independent of philosophy. Zombie-meaning is a product of the same mindless process. And I do mean *mindless*, both in the sense that the process is without a mind of its own and that it requires an absence of mind to do its thing. The average man has no idea how exposed he is to intellectual subjugation as he lets it happen.

I assure you, many are willing to capitalize on the opportunity. Concept is the most important spoil for anyone aspiring to gain influence over people. It has been the prize jewel in which pursuit were created such tools as propaganda, political and economic alike. It is the reason that mass education has made people stupider en masse. It has been the cause of extremism in some instances and apathy in others. It has been a thing to either assimilate or eliminate – never left to the free will of the people.

But there is no epic conspiracy of a single mindset: conceptual paradigms are not owned by a small minority. Nor are they forced upon people outside of openly totalitarian regimes. Rather, there are as many conceptual paradigms as there are convenient truths, and they are as varied as the sum of a speaker's personal preferences. Men's acceptance of whatever they (generally unconsciously) choose is not so much a centralized conspiracy, but something akin to the enrollment in a cult. This is why so many appear devoted to misunderstanding – it is not stupidity, but faith; it is not insanity, but loyalty; nor is it a lack of sociability that has been the cause of the alienation we witness at present, but a rise of sectarianism.

The Age of Cultism

Historians like to map the temporal dimensionality of our species in demarcated instances of societal character; borders drawn according to dominant trend, emergent thought, perceived purpose, imposed doctrine, and recorded practice. As far as everyone can agree, there has been a general age associated with stone, and three ages known for metal. As far as most people agree, this has given way to antiquity, the Middle Ages, the pre-modern era, the modern era, and whatever we have now. A slightly deeper dive into the division would reveal a Hellenistic era and a Roman era, a Christian era and *the dark ages*, an age of enlightenment and an age of romanticism (if you are into literature), slavery feudalism and democracy (if you are a Marxist), and a steel and a gunpowder era (if you are a nerd). There have been at least four ages of empires and at most one age of information. Please do not take this paragraph for a serious lesson in history by the way; that is not its purpose. There are many époques for which one can argue, many standards on which to base them, and many reasons to deny them as unreliably one-dimensional. There is a degree of nominal liberty in all categorization. The division of history is just fictional enough to allow for many creative fictions in the observation of mankind's many manifestations through time. It is this poeticism of the past that has given me the idea to argue what I write next.

The 19th century is known as the *Age of Nationalism*. It was the first instance in which the concept of nations as we recognize them today became the dominant fashion across Europe. This was the latest trend, purpose, and aspiration: to draw borders, to establish identity, to fantasize about ethnogenesis; to trace continuity to the glorious origins of an ethnie, to weed out the less glorious blood, and to do away with all inglorious blood; to come up with concepts corresponding to *who* in regards to subject and object, and a concept of *why* in reference to the verb. It was seldom a just verb. The values of the previous era were jettisoned to make room for this new dynamic. The values of the era before the previous era were jettisoned twice over. Remnants of epochs when people recognized one another as noblemen or peasants, as citizens or barbarians, Christian or heathen, Protestant or Catholic, educated or simple, or victims or what-have-you, were all assimilated into the new supraethnicity of the nation: former citizens of the same empire were now nationals of hostile countries; in a religious state, one's faith was the national church, (or if the state was irreligious, the church was an enemy of the state), the Christianity of foreign nations being, of course, a Christianity of a variably inferior God, on occasion heretical; and an educated person from one country was considered an uneducated rube in another. This much is mostly accepted in the historical record. The Age of Nationalism was supplanted in the middle of the twentieth century by what I will here call the Age of Ideology,[30] by which the West came to regard what were formerly distinct nations as either Communists or the good guys, and the East regarded formerly distinct nations as Soviet or the bad guys. Ethnicities, borders, and historiography were all concepts to be tailored according to this new division. What we study as history today is largely a consequence of convenient narrative surrounding the Cold War. Education was cut to measure. They had to make it fit. Religion did not avoid the trend either: the East just about outlawed it, and the West introduced the doctrine that a good Christian was an unrepentant Capitalist.

I set up this foundation to argue for what we see happening now, as I notice we have been experiencing yet another change in epochs. I was originally going to call it The Age of Business, as it seems as though people are expected to alter their convictions according to the economy; to betray their countries if it means business, to make communist merchandize if it sells, to print Bibles and put them in bookstores with erotic fiction. None of these are hypothetical examples by the way. I thought I was on the right track, as I have been hearing, increasingly frequently, the all too common argument, reworded with decreasing eloquence, that an immorality committed for money is not an immorality. But there was still something that I could not explain by dubbing this new epoch a mere *Age of Business*. It was the fact of mass disassociation.

The fact that people are becoming increasingly alienated from their friends, families, and, in the most perfected stage, estranged

---

[30] I am also tempted to call it the age of simplification.

from reality altogether. Business alone cannot account for this. There have always been rich people, but the relatively recent depletion of social cohesion is nonetheless *recent*; a cult of mammon alone cannot account for it. Nor can the cult of mammon in isolation account for the complete divorce from reality I see all over – especially among people who do not care to be particularly wealthy. While my initial theory explained some of it, it was not the full picture. I could not make sense of conservative Christians defending pornographers, of socialist atheists supporting the monopolization of science, of spiritual gurus relying on bodily toxins, financially situated families falling apart, First World countries resembling anything but, mentally deranged intellectuals, the prominence of PR firms, the popularization of narrative over truth... No, a cult of mammon cannot suffice the totality of the emerging trend. But perhaps the answer to suffice is not an upgrade, but a subtraction. Perhaps my initial theory was mistaken in that it was only 150% correct. It was a sin of excess. I had overdefined it. I was not looking at a Cult of Mammon. I was merely looking at a cult – one of many.

I often employ a metaphor of cult-worship to explain unyielding adherence to ignoble ideas – the referential scope of *idea* being on the gross side of enormous. *The Playwright* is largely about that.[31] In as far as a cult is a religious sect, religion is an organized set of beliefs and practices, and a sect is an exclusive fellowship, to liken blind adherence to membership in a cult is to use the word with so strong a resonance that it is a virtually literal employment of the expression.

The more specific a definition one tries to assign to the concept of cult to hopefully differentiate it from the metaphor, the more prominent the similarities between the two become. Any attempt to narrow it down exclusively to spiritual religion is an attempt to detract from the meaning of the word, not to specify its true

---

[31] Then again, it is about many things (it is postmodernist to no end).

meaning. You can tell this because there are such things as *cults of personality* which are perfectly secular. The argument that a cult entails an overtly passionate devotion, of the kind you see mostly in film, is also a poor argument. The only people to accept it are people who have never gone to school with a party-girl Jehovah's Witness dating a hooligan, or have not been familiarized with the Mormon concept of soaking (lucky them).

Any loyalty to an ideational whole without adequate reason is symptomatic of cultism. It does not matter if you joined for salvation or for financial gain, if you worship Dagon or your employer, or if you sacrifice your blood or your ethics. It does not even matter if you pray daily or if you are only partially indoctrinated in custom. As long as you are ideationally unyielding and practically loyal to your conviction, you are following a cult. You do not even have to be aware of it. It is pointless to try and downplay the fact. You are *hardly even a sympathizer*, you think to yourself, *let alone a member*. After all, your allegiance is only a lukewarm acceptance of the system – not a passionate conviction! You merely drink Jim's Juice in Jonestown to make your boss happy; you know full well it will not get you to heaven.

So is everything a cult then? Not at all. The most important way in which a cult differs from a proper ideology is that a cult is, by definition, wrong in its conception of reality. This wrongness is generally easy to notice: no system of belief with a claim on reality can have in its foundation traces of hypocrisy, contradiction, profit, intimidation, coercion, mindlessness, recklessness, malice, deception, or segregation. A good thing is something you ought to share – so segregation has obviously no claim on reality; honesty is the chief virtue of transcribing reality, and so, hypocrisy and deception do not belong; this is inseparable from sound reasoning, which forbids contradiction, mindlessness and recklessness; a real ideology accepts truth for no other reason than that it is true, by which such things as profit, intimidation and coercion cannot be representative of reality; and the problem of malice goes without saying.

Selectivity is the second important differentiator between cult-like behavior and honest ideational adherence. A cultist will not have his beliefs challenged, so he will stay away from potential challengers – he will either remove himself from them (when he has no power) or remove them from his surroundings (when he does have power); if he has absolute power, he will try to shut them up completely. The third qualifier is the inability to change one's mind on the subject. It is the absence of a functional conceptual filter. An honest man considers concept a thing to be refined and improved, a thing to measure and to determine; a cultist holds to concept without care for refinement or improvement. This is because the final element of cultism is the conviction of ownership of a piece of heaven – the assurance of virtue, the assurance of perfection, and the assurance of having gained it.

<u>A Fable, Three Methods and Double the Flaws</u>

To ward against wild beasts, the gods gave man teeth and nails. To keep safe from the deception of demons, they blessed man with superior intellect. And to ensure he does not go astray, they gave him a sense of righteousness. They threw in a coat of fur to make sure he is warm in the winter. As they looked down upon their creation, they realized they had made a mistake. What was supposed to be their beautiful creation looked rather like a monster, with teeth and nails and all covered in fur. *Scrap the wild traits*, the chief deity suggested – *man has superior intellect, he will figure out how to keep warm and defend himself without them.* What we call evolution was an aesthetic choice. As they regarded their creation a second time, they noticed their second mistake right away: their beautiful creation was thinking too much, and was therefore not at all concerned with its own beauty. *Curtail the mind*, the chief deity ordered – *man's righteousness will keep him safe from evil!* What we call superficiality was by design an update. Their third glance at their beautiful creation, however, left the gods in a state of penitence, as they realized their third error. Their labor of beauty was going extinct, for man had become pathologically altruistic. *Let man grow a little wicked*, the chief deity admonished his servants – *for he is now too stupid to understand heroism, and just gullible enough to misunderstand mercy!* It was then that deceitful demons, having fallen long before man was created, and apt to steal from the gods their beautiful creation, ventured to lead man astray, and, having succeeded now that man had no sense of justice by which to keep his path, they provoked the wrath of the gods, who had just then realized that their beautiful creation had become the property of another. To avenge the swindle, the deity in charge made the following decision: *man is not deserving of beauty, for beauty is exclusively of the gods, and if one is not of the gods, one must ever remain ugly – ugly, I say, ugly as sin!* Since then, man has walked about the earth as he does now: with an unimpressive excuse for teeth nails and hair, suitable for nothing but painting and brushing, a semblance of intellect, getting things too wrong to ever evolve beyond a semblance, and a trace of righteousness, by which we know but two things: there is good and bad, and we prefer the latter more often than it is reasonable. Throughout all of this, we have the unshakeable notion that we ought to be beautiful, but that we really aren't; that ugliness is a sin, and that a beautiful person can never be truly evil; that we must look pretty lest we are tried as demons, and that, if we are ever seen in the presence of demons, we had best convince the person who saw us that our particular demon is actually beautiful.

You laugh, but if I pretended that this was an ancient Sumerian legend, I could have moved on to demonstrate how the myth has influenced the mythology of the Middle East, how it has made its way into European tradition, and how we witness its cultural ripples in the present day. If I had done a good enough job, it would have read like an excerpt of anthropological genius. As it stands, I cannot cite it as a piece of ancient wisdom, so it will remain a mostly jocular introduction to this next subject.

And as I make the joke, one must keep in mind that comedy is not incompatible with reality. There really is, in the modern day, an obsession with beauty, impossible standards for beauty, and utter ignorance in regards the meaning of that word. I do not suppose I am likely to meet any disagreement there. Yet, this is not the only truth to be taken out of the story. Another truth, which it shares with every other myth for that matter, is that man, universally, has an innate urge to explain the world around him, regardless of the era and regardless of his education. There has always been the drive to make sense of the observable universe. Else, we would not be in the position to know so much about mythology – there would be nobody to study myth, and nobody to have created it in the first place. It is all in our gift to make up stories and apply them to reality. Stories like the one the ancients made up specifically for this chapter are called myths. Even in science, theories are just the kind of stories we tell. Let me accentuate then, that as long as a story (be it narrative poetic or scientific) can be said to have any trace of truth in it, and as long as an individual can determine what it is, this trace, once recognized, and followed to its conclusion, will inevitably bring us closer to a truth that really does reveal something essential about the workings of the universe. This is what fantasy is all about. It is about seeing things that are not there, measuring them to things that are, and deciding which parts to keep. It is such a reliable method of learning and teaching that we entrust kids with it. It is such a quality method that we take pleasure in it even as adults. It is among the earliest incarnations of the cartographer. There will always be something to hear (an echo, by chance), we will always desire to make sense of what we have heard, and we will (almost) always get at least some of it right, as even a syllable points to the full word. And it is the means by which one goes about this that I want to discuss next.

The first means is the conceptual filter. It is the independent pursuit of truth. It is man making sense of the world according to what he sees in the world, provided he can see and has the time to make sense of it. It is the bootstrap method and the most self-assuring of the lot. But the line between confidence and stupidity is not necessarily an uninterrupted delineation. This method, like most methods, cannot be practiced with an assurance of flawlessness. The first flaw, being that a man may be wrong in his attempt to make sense of reality, is more natural law than potential peril – like rejection in the pursuit of romance, the only people not to have experienced it are people who have not ventured to pursue it. We have only so many opportunities to acquire knowledge independently, and only so much intellectual willpower at a time. But mistake is not the only shortcoming of this method, for even if we could make the right conclusions without deviation, those would still be too limited in number to matter a whole deal by the fact of our mortality. A method for learning entirely dependent on the person doing the learning is impractical even without hurdles. You can only acquire so much knowledge, and you can only keep it for so long. What's more, you would not want to let it go to waste.

This is why we have the second means of learning, which is learning by trust. We trust others to teach us. *Others* could refer to any number of individuals, and any method of teaching, be it direct or indirect, or the combination of the two that we call tradition – tradition especially so, in as far as tradition is the historical agreement of individuals continuing into the collective present. This is not a matter of uncritical compliance. It is the enabler of genius. The average physicist today is more knowledgeable on the subject of physics than Nikola Tesla was in his time. Regarding tradition, TS Eliot remarked that we know so much more than our predecessors only because they partake in "that which we know." It is the greatest advantage of the system of trust. We are lucky to have been taught things since we were young enough to learn, and so by people competent enough to teach us. The first flaw of this system is self-evident: it trains potential overreliance on *people competent enough to teach us.* Just like the individuals that contribute to it, tradition is often wrong. But even if there were such a thing as we can consistently trust without the risk of it teaching us poorly, we would have no means of figuring out what it is – out of a multitude of teachers, it is hard to pick out the ideal master when you have no knowledge on the subject.

Hence, the institute of authority as the third means of learning. Authority differs from trust in that trust is a decision contingent on the student (the one who does the learning), whereas authority depends on the one from whom the student learns. You choose to trust people and tradition, but you do not choose an authority on the subject; you may choose to distrust the source, but this says nothing of its holding a position of authority. The upside to this is that it allows for consistent specialization – individuals are allowed to learn specific subjects, they have an easier time choosing which individuals to trust, and they are granted the privilege of being trusted to further the existing base of knowledge. Authority does not even have to be an individual; authority can be a prior study, a proven method, or even the authority of one's own senses. What authority really stands for is a suggested systematization of trust. The first downside, you have guessed the pattern by now, is that authority can be mistaken. The second downside is that, even if there is such a thing as an authority that never errs, and even if we were presented with this inerrant authority, we would have no reason to trust ourselves to have trusted the right authority, seeing as we did not come by this knowledge independently; it was handed down to us not because of our own decision, but an external order, explicit or otherwise: *this is how it is, and you don't get a say in it. Your ability to think for yourself might have never existed.* Even if true, it does not inspire confidence. A full dedication to authority as a means of making sense of the world is an implicit admittance that one is incapable of making sense of the world.

The three means make up a balance of figuring things out on one's own, choosing to trust some sources, and trusting others on the shorthand of authority. Where personal assessment will not suffice, trusting another will. Where trust is not enough, systematic trust will turn the perilous leap of faith into a safer leap of faith – as long as it is our own decision, that is. I cannot stress this enough: if we are to get anywhere, we must be in the position where we trust ourselves to trust others. Which is all the more reason to keep the wisdom of the ancient Sumerians in consideration. Because the fall of man, according to that ancient tale, was not a deception exploiting an isolated instance of stupidity, but the demonic swindle that took place as mankind lost his sense of righteousness. Now, that we no longer feel an obligation to be just, nor do we see why others would feel such an obligation, the means of acquiring knowledge have become corrupted: we cannot trust ourselves to trust anyone.

The myth, written so long ago and in so distant a land, narrated that the last thing the gods confiscated from mankind was his beauty, so that he may resemble the demons all the more, seeing as he had chosen them as his new masters. We no longer have the favor of the gods. And yet, what on first glance might seem a narcissistic decision on the part of the chief deity, might just prove the thing that saves us from total destruction; because, being ugly as sin, and knowing our neighbor to be no more attractive than ourselves, we have been permitted a saving shred of wisdom, in that we do not trust our kind in totality for the same reason we do not trust those hideous demons either. The pride that marked *their* fall, many eons prior to our own, is not an actor in our damnation, at least not inherently: we are not nearly good-looking clean and elegant enough to fool ourselves with it (not for long, at least; and not in the sincerity of our intimate doubts). Like the demons, we are repulsive, but unlike the demons, we still remember we were meant to be beautiful; so we sense no elating righteousness in our damnation, but a humbling reflection as we look in the mirror. And it just might be this bit of modesty that restores some of our means of learning – of our gift of intellect, clearly diminished, but still functional: we are modest enough to trust modest people. Moreover, we are modest enough to distrust the man who is not. The man who, so resembling the beast in so many ways, now venturing to resemble him in ambition as well, and on occasion wealthy enough to conceal his ugliness, is not Adonis of the gods come in lieu of Prometheus, but of the banks the PR departments the plastic surgeons and a demonic conviction, come to hijack our means of learning, and to tell us *this is how it is, and you don't get a say in it; your ability to make sense of the world might have as well never existed!*

The Fourth Minister

This is the threat to liberty. The longer we neglect it, the more will we find ourselves outnumbered by those who know very little, and, by example, bolster the case against critical thinking. Do forsake any and all notions of a threat to liberty such that cannot be divorced from politics. That liberty has been made the subject exclusively of socio-political humdrum is a sign the concept is on the verge of zombification. A thriving economy is proof of a free population no more than wealth in a family is proof of a happy family. Nor is the question of *who is in charge*, on the same tangent, any more relevant to the happiness of a family, provided the one who has been entrusted to be in charge is good, and provided those who have entrusted him to be good are willing to put their trust into action. You may draw the political parallel as you please. The threat to liberty is independent of politics in the long term. Liberty thrives in concord and harmony and direction – you remember the wings (88). The opposite is slavery – ideological, personal, social (all of them). I have no doubt that there will, in all likelihood, eventually arrive a literal tyrant to swoop down and take advantage of this discord with a political dictatorship. But he is a product, not the cause of our slavery. He might root for it and try to hurry it along its way, but the original cause will always be discord, enmity, and stupidity.

There are three ministers presently hard at work to take advantage of the crisis: to bolster it or to facilitate it; to pave the way for the prime minister once the majority has consented to the installation of their buttons. I admit, the word minister here is an Orwellian reference. I was originally hesitant to employ the metaphor, seeing as talking about *1984* has become something of a cliché, however, I have at last come to believe that this is all the more reason to talk about it. When the definitive, easily-accessible, well-written, unambiguous, and eerily predictive handbook on tyranny is being, by the argument of its alleged overuse, discouraged from address regarding the powers that might be, I am inclined to look upon it not as a cliché, but as censorship by pretension. In that sense, I believe it is more a pseudointellectual position to avoid it for the sake of avoiding ridicule than to actively sustain it in our collective memory; let the hyenas cackle if they will. I will now proceed to describe the three ministers of truth that prey on misunderstanding for their mischievous ends: the Null Tyrant, the Authoritative Tyrant, and the Idiomatic Tyrant. None of them are specific human beings, but behaviors – behaviors arising out of convictions, and convictions of conceptual conquest: to preside over our right to know reality, and the means by which we come by this knowledge.

Now, the first minister of truth, the Null Tyrant, is the conviction that there is no need to know things. Alternatively, among his intellectual serfs, the belief that misunderstanding is such an inherent part of life, and a person so unlikely to know all that much, that it is best that a man does not seek to know anything – not anything beyond the immediately applicable. Many people serve him. In the majority, it is probably just a case of laziness. In the rest, it is some poor attempt at enlightenment. In both cases, it is the quickest road to cognitive chaos. It is for this same reason, however, that it tends to backfire. The Null Tyrant is not the drive to establish an overarching meaning; it is not a conquering general. Hence, its impressive speed. It is a sheer destructive force; a vandal raider. The conviction does not seek to impose itself as anything definite. It only seeks to eliminate meaning or the faith in it. It is why it is most commonly used as a vanguard for the other two ministers, seeing as it is, on principle, not capable of anything beyond ruin. It is only a tyrant officially; otherwise, it is just an executioner.

I have witnessed it in action. There was a time when we were being told to relax and not care about things; to embrace hedonism, to shun realism, to flip an unrighteous finger to self-righteous tradition. This was the subversion of the previous code, an authoritarian affair of being taught to worry all throughout the first decade of schooling. If at an earlier point we were being told to stay away from drugs, our sophomore year in college saw a condoning of opiates that at times bordered on direct encouragement. The values we learned in childhood were best left in childhood, we were told. If our first grade teachers sought to make us hardworking pupils, college professors taught us that hard work and learning and whatnot really is nothing and what-have-you. The most valuable thing in the world was to learn that there are no such things as values. In the same setting, but nearing the point of backfire: if in the first grade we all knew that politicians were liars and thieves and really dishonest people with fake smiles, by the time we got to college, we had authority figures on campus tell us which politicians will save the country (and possibly the world) and movements that we had best support if we at all cared to save the country (or the world) or at least cared to get a favorable grade. I suppose you can tell how well this went. Nobody cared to support anybody. We did not care to save a bad world that did not even matter, nor did we care to get a good grade now that grades did not matter either. After all, we had come to shun realism (political realism no less) for we were told that there is no truth, and we had come to distrust authority as we were taught to distrust authority. A drugged-up sex-crazed generation flipping an unrighteous finger is not much of a political force behind which to rally a movement. It is capable of hatred, for one's political enemies not least, but hatred does not discriminate. Among my friends, the most promiscuous drug-abusing liberally-minded hater of the patriarchy was in fierce enmity with the most pro-promiscuity drug-supporting liberally-minded activist against the patriarchy – the former had zero tolerance for self-righteousness, including that of her self-claimed ally; she was in it for the high and hump, not the protests and the voting booths. The latter, by contrast, could not tolerate people who refused to follow her, even if they agreed in principle. No, the first minister cannot recruit an army; he only leaves ruins. He has no intention whatsoever of building an empire and making himself Caesar. He is a tyrant in name only.

The second minister is more nuanced than that. The second minister is the Authoritative Tyrant. He understands the need for authority too well, and he knows how to exploit it. He is authoritative to no end, and, on that note, he is the most annoying of the lot. We may call him an Aristocrat. Those of us who did, by some miracle remain sober, and owing to this managed not to succumb to the Null Tyrant, got to make the acquaintance of the Aristocrat. We were exposed to the mentality that is the Authoritative Tyrant as we began to dabble in academic work, having previously graduated from an academia that had, just a bit earlier, argued that it was not a very important institution, as it presently sought to convince us that it is the most important factor in society other than the politicians our support for whom was to secure the fate of the country and the world and don't forget our grades. The Authoritative Tyrant is the fallacy of appeal to authority – systematized, institutionalized, and imposed as the quintessential element in argument. One cannot write a paper without it. One cannot cite a source lacking it. One cannot oppose a source that contains it. It is the established canon on truth.

I have already addressed this aspect of academia in "The Emaciation of Intellect."[32] There, I argued against one-sided peer reviews and made some remarks against the academic obsession with cited sources. In short, I summarized the latter aspect of

---

[32] It is the opening essay to *Chapbook #3* of *The Chapbooks Trilogy;*

intellectual gatekeeping as "a tool of indoctrination, railroading thought, discouraging independent thought, and tracking influences in the case of dissenting thought" (66). You can tell a lot about a person by the sources they use. For one, the literature one reads will accurately tell you how compliant they are without requiring a straining deal of effort on your end; the last page of my paper will tell you if we are *on the same page*. If you dislike the authors I cite, you can dismiss the entirety of my text on account of my sources. None of the original arguments I have proposed during my academic involvement have ever faced actual academic criticism. Whenever I have argued for something outside the norm, the attack has always been against my sources or lack thereof. Note, I did not necessarily disagree with the norm – I merely said something other than a reiteration of it, and the hive mind retaliated. I do not deny that citing sources is an important part of any piece of non-fiction. With that, citations exist to "credit a point, validate a statement, or debate a claim. They do not exist to be forced into each paragraph, whether needed or not, nor do they exist for authors to be bullied into having them, again, whether needed or not." I am sure that, if an academician were to read that sentence, he would ask me for the source. I am tired of hearing *Who said this?* regarding my own original propositions.

But that aside, consider the chapter a few pages back, where I talked about the Age of Cultism. Imagine if I had cited sources on the theoretical bases by which historical epochs are demarcated: that the Age of Nationalism is called that because of an obsession with nationalism, or the latest papers refuting or substantiating this claim, or that there really were three ages known for metal (not counting the 1980's), or the historical peer-reviewed evidence over which I italicized *the dark ages* as a joke. You would have seen a string of text by a different author contained in each sentence, a lot of quotation marks and parentheses to credit them, information on which page of which generic textbook you would not care to pick up contains them, and not one bit of additional meaning in my paragraph to validate the wasted time, ink, and paper. My text would look sloppier, and none the more informative for it. Without that waste, however, academia will not care for the argument I make further into the chapter. *How can we even trust the author about an age of cultism?!* they would ask, rhetorically, *when he is so irreverent of our institution, he has not cared to assure us that the words he utters have been previously approved by one of our own?!*

This is not exclusive to academia, by the way. The average citizen also prefers sources over common sense, logical argument, or experience. He imitates academicians hoping to look smart. In other cases, not concerned with faking intellect, he bows to other forms of authority, such as his social circle, a domineering friend, or people he sees on TV; recently, I have been hearing appeals to the law or *the system* in this same manner. The Aristocrat, though prone to hijacking highbrow circles, is not exclusively of the intellectual camp.

I just find it funny how pronounced it is in academia, an institution that should, if there is any merit to their intellectual authority, know better than to appeal to authority. The case is made worse by the single-blindness of the peer-review process. For more on the subject, you can look into "The Emaciation of Intellect" – please do. For now, suffice it to say that it allows the peer-reviewer to be as unfair as they please, and the person being peer-reviewed is given no means to protest against unfair criticism. In this sense, it really does resemble a political tyranny, with a very literal ministry of truth. *You do not have ministry-approved text, therefore, you will not be approved by the ministry.*

Now, do not misunderstand me – I will say it again: it is important to cite sources; knowledge is a virtue, and that of former studies on your subject is an aid; research is the better part of learning; real scientists do it all the time. But the thing about real scientists is that they will not dismiss an argument just because it does not pay homage to the canon. The difference between the proper use of citations and an appeal to authority is that a real scholar cites sources intending to introduce something other than his sources, whereas a subject of the fallacy cites sources intending to cover his lack of contribution. If the former asks for a source, it is out of curiosity – if he recommends a source, it is to help enrich an argument; when the latter asks for a source, he does it hoping to avoid an argument (or an arguer) he dislikes; when he suggests there should be citations, he only means to shame.

And do not mistake an inconsistently high standard for an actual high standard. If we stack cardboard boxes and paint them matte gray, it will be only the illusion of a sturdy wall. It may convince some people that it really is the front of a fortress, but those who are in on the scam know it will not survive a siege. It is why they avoid defensive scenarios, hoping to deter opposition by intimidation rather than man those brittle battlements; it is why the gatekeeper is so strict about who he lets in. You must be sworn in before you are entrusted with the secret. The standard of established literature is just canonized fashion. Theories regarded as the scientific consensus are largely preferred trends, generally by ideology, on occasion by convenience, with cherry-picked facts and tolerated fabrications.

But its elitism is also why it too tends to backfire. Because, once the means for acquiring knowledge have become so constrained, and *learned* people have turned that adjective into heredity (to the point of inbreeding), the only people capable of preaching to this choir are people who are paid to learn the lyrics and the melody and to sing in the same choir. The aristocrat can only impose himself in an aristocracy. Otherwise, he may as well be a pretentiously robed professor pretentiously droning on about whatever pretentiously robed professors drone on about. Ironically, the attempt to impose such rigid authority over knowledge has only further discouraged the average person's interest in learning, and has instead nudged him to regard academic institutions, now with their authoritarianism so brazenly stated, as all the less deserving of his trust. What's more, in the Age of Cultism, this has done little for the subjugation of the masses under one tyrant; on the contrary, it has spawned multiple cult leaders playing aristocrat in their own segregated cults. It seems as though the Authoritative Tyrant is less competent even than his Null cousin. At least the latter is capable of total destruction. This one is incapable of any totality, let alone total rule.

And its failure is largely due to the third minister, which is the Idiomatic Tyrant. He is the most powerful so far. He is the leader of each cult. He is the prison warden. He is every one of us. He is self-serving ambition, personal conviction, arrogance, greed, self-righteousness, you know all about him. We all do. It is the force behind the man with the doctorate who is always right, the thing that makes the mechanic loathe educators because they do not understand cars, that belief among the powerful that they are above morality. "It is quite the petty game we play: to make ourselves look good by the people we condemn. To make ourselves feel sane compared to the rest" ("Pythagoras' Prison" 28). He is the inner ear most attuned to the broken echo.

It took me until only recently (very recently) to come to terms with just how little people care for reality. I used to think that those who err with full conviction are really fooled by a false conviction; it was somewhat of a shock to come to a place where I could no longer put my optimism before the real issue: those who err with full conviction could not care less if their conviction is true or false.

Just about everybody has his own spin on reality, and it is anchored in his personal spin on superiority. This is the Idiomatic Tyrant. The Madman. He could commit a crime in front of you and lie to your face about it and feel blameless over it, not because he thinks he has fooled you, nor because he has fooled himself, but because he knows you cannot do anything about it. It is because of this third minister that the other two can actualize, and it is also because of him that they cannot advance one step beyond their initial conquest. He is division. He is individualism minus reality. As such, though his role is essential for the invasion, he is not quite the one to cause the unification of villainy – the kind that will completely eradicate the individual, or advance alienation into annihilation. At most, he will account for a completely hostile congregation of individuals; there is worse to come. Yes, the madman builds a madhouse for his fortress, but at least we all have our individual madnesses. You can be Napoleon if I can be Julius Caesar; you can even be Brutus as long as you have got yourself a different Caesar. As the third minister is given his way with humanity, we are in a state just shy of hell. It is certainly not a good place to be. Still, it is hell that I have promised you – not the pre-hell you can already surmise for yourselves. And I mean to deliver.

That is why the fourth minister is such an insidious being. The creation of this hell is his specialty. The one thing that will direct all of the ministers to the same goal; every perversion, every dictatorial urge that aims to subjugate reality will find its most potent ally in this great unifier: the notion that reality cannot be known and is therefore not worth contemplating, the notion that reality belongs to an institution, and the notion that reality can be whatever we need it to be – they have at last found a king to rule over them and by whom to rule; the Raider, the Aristocrat, and the Madman, their many differences complementing instead of opposing one another, the weaknesses by which they would normally fall no longer such a drawback. It will be an authority under which all bend, even if they are too proud to bow. He is the most powerful tool of the prime minister yet.

Imagine a dispute between two people. One of them makes an argument. The other does not care to consider the argument. He merely inserts his collocutor's message into a machine, and asks of the machine to make him a counterargument. The machine does as instructed. Its master then, not caring much for the content of the counterargument, sends this generated reply to his collocutor. He has done his part. Do you see it now? He has not cared to learn anything about reality, he has handed over his trust entirely to the authority of the machine, and he has remained convinced that he is correct because he holds himself to be the arbiter of truth. The ministers – all three, as one. As if this were not absurd enough as it is, his collocutor will do the exact same thing. The machine will comply. They will both be in disagreement over different answers given to them by the same authority – divided by their ambition and united by their master; a master of chaos and of authority alike.

For the longest time, this machine used to be a venerated abstract kind of authority – popular science, mass media, *great men* in contemporary history... So far, they have been mostly limited in their scope, and they have depended to an extent on an involvement of both parties. But now, it really is a machine on which people rely to make their arguments. A writer and an artist, and a few other things directly threatened by the emergence of artificial intelligence, I make no secret of the fact that I have every incentive to oppose the technology. But I do not write from a position of professional self-preservation. I will reserve the full-scale attack against AI for my next essay (or part of it). In regards to human misunderstanding, artificial intelligence is not a threat to my job – it is a threat to humanity altogether. The problem was never its emerging sentience or its access to nuclear codes or whatever else cheap science-fiction will make into an episode. The problem is its promotion into a conceptual processor, and the regression of persons into organic mechanisms – inelegant automata or flesh-calculators.

This illusion of intelligence is trying to disqualify the thinking man, while emphasizing his qualification for a sack of flesh reacting to prompts. I warn you again, though you should expect it by now, not to read that literally – qualification is not about your job. You may still keep your job as a professor or a writer or a journalist. You will very likely keep your job as a doctor, and definitely your job as a janitor. What you will lose is what you have begun to lose already – your status as a thinking person; as somebody capable of thinking for themselves, of coming to correct conclusions, challenging the narrative, changing your mind, changing the minds of others, acquiring your own bit of knowledge by your own effort, your own decisions, and your own free will. The concept of the human being, the rational animal, has been put in jeopardy, as it is not exclusively personhood, but also circuitry, that now appears capable of matching the set. Humanity has run its course; all that is left now is the regurgitated sum of its past.

I am not in a minority position as I argue this. Even lukewarm proponents of artificial intelligence technology will assent that AI is safe as long as we use it in moderation, which implies that its safety is conditional at best. It is sad, their pleading: AI is safe as long we don't go overboard with it, of course, as long as we use it as far as we use it and no more until we use it as much as we will be using it the more we use it – but only for good, of course, because that is how the world works. It is like discovering that cocaine can boost confidence and then arguing for its widespread use – of course, only in moderation. We have taken something that is not intelligence and called it intelligence, we have taken something that does not think and called it a superior thinker, and, the peak of absurdity, though we judge it to have outpaced us in our most prominent qualities, we insist that we can control it. We make fallacies within fallacies. I am not worried about the superiority of artificial intelligence; it is not superior. I am rather worried about how stupid we have become to trust ourselves with trusting a flawed creation by a proud designer. We have chosen a universal *yes-man* to always be our *yes-man* provided we are also its *yes-men*.

This is all very hard to argue. Many people still consider it too vague to make sense. What's more, I cannot denounce artificial intelligence if we have not yet settled the meaning of natural intelligence – above all, of *human* intelligence. Which is just as well, because defining intelligence is an important step away from confusion, and closer to understanding and potentially concord and by chance an intelligent redirection. AI by itself is not as scary as the fact that the concept of intelligence has also undergone zombification. So I will leave the robot for my next essay. For now, I will try to argue for the meaning of intelligence – what is it, who has it, and why we need it.

The only side with a valid claim on truth is the side that is characterized by this distinctly human quality. So we had better revive the concept and learn to use it. I believe us to have it, and I believe us to be its masters. The alternative is to become as artificial as the artificial plant we are mistaking for superior nature.

The Right to Reality

<u>What Intelligence Isn't</u>

It was over a relatively recent fad online that I began to contemplate the subject of human intelligence in more detail than I had until then cared to dedicate to the matter. My most recent brush with the subject prior to the article in question was an affair that was, at the time, interesting only to my postmodernist recollection, in its jubilant defeatism, which in retrospect must have been providential, much to the confusion of my postmodernist conditioning, for it is a story which interpretative two-sidedness will provide a soft conclusion to the chapter I am presently writing, so long after the fact, with a twist that approaches a screwball comedy. I first learned about that term from Dean Koontz, and I find it relevant here for his description stating that characters should be "largely unaware of the way in which they leave the male lead in a state of perpetual confusion… propelled by surprising character twists and revelations that delight us and that are *logical within the given structure of the story*" (337). While there are other elements to screwball comedy, most of which align with the event I am about to reference, and though some of them require too wide a stretch to make it, having specified of the event that it only *approaches* a screwball comedy, the most prominent elements align perfectly, not excluding the twist by which the apparent airhead "turns out, in the end, to be the wisest of all the characters."

The memory in question, to put it in context, is of a mandatory intelligence test included in the health exam required for getting a driver's license. The people who have so far disagreed with me in this essay will be happy to know that I scored average. I have already lost the debate to the 115s and aboves. They have no need to read on, for they have proven their intellect already, and I have gambled mine away with my *coming out.*

The licensed professional handed me my copy. The instructions were to look at the image at the top of each question and match it to an identical image out of several options below. Every question was to be answered using the same technique: see the image, find its match, and circle it. I was not halfway done with the second page before the professional with a Ph.D. took my papers, wrote *average*, and sent me on my way. I wondered at the time what hidden genius-clause in the test I must have missed to become doomed to mediocrity. Then again, I never knew I was supposed to look for one. I could not stay and ask questions, however; I had to take an eye exam and a psychological exam immediately after. The optometrist complimented my sight. I have always been proud of my elven vision, though I do not think this particular test was quite what it should have been. For one, the optometrist was an otorhinolaryngologist. Of the holes in the head, his specialty were all of them *except* the eyes. The psychologist who may have been a psychiatrist or a neurologist hit me with a hammer in three of my extremities (at least one quarter of me is to this day untested) and asked me no questions regarding my compulsiveness, my intrusive thoughts, or my opinion on pineapple on pizza. I was as of that point considered ready to drive. I even got to skip the blood test as the employees were nice enough to take me at my word. I am not making up any of this. It is not even a bad thing – self-conscious *pro forma* makes for less grueling experiences with mandated formalities than does the professionalism of conscientious bureaucrats.

People passionate about testing intelligence might be, expectedly, disappointed. The proof of my stupidity was really not a valid test. But I will make another point that will further annoy the camp of measurable intelligence: it was not just this test of intelligence that was not valid – all tests of intelligence are equally as bull. It is just that, to build up to the screwball conclusion, the people in my story knew this already, so they could not care less for the charade of *proper* testing, in either intelligence or any of the other metrics: as long as you can read the numbers, you can see well enough – an optometrist would be wasting his talents on you; as long as you look sufficiently sane, a psychologist's time would be better employed on the novella on his desk. Most importantly, as long as you can follow simple instructions, you are smart enough to drive. Any assessment of genius beyond that is no more an indicator of a future Nobel Prize than it is of three failed driving exams. The inclusion of a sciency metric is just for show.

The most commonly accepted measure, which terminology, threateningly professional in formal contexts and boorishly simplified in informal use, is the standardized IQ-test, which pins the person taking the test on a spectrum between idiot and genius, with a few variations in between, all in reference to other people who have taken that same test. It tests one's ability to memorize on the spot and to see patterns: visual, mathematical, linguistic, and logical (but chiefly visual and mathematical). The scores derived this way, it is argued, have shown a positive correlation between people's IQ scores and their success in life – their jobs, their income, their intellectual output (whatever that means), etc. There are so many flaws in the very conception of such a system, that it is almost hard to believe we are even debating it. Alas, there are people who take these tests to be the definitive statement on intelligence – not only do they consider the code cracked, but they proceed to argue for an intellectual determinism by its cypher.

I know the arguments that come up in its defense. *IQ tests do measure (at least) something and (at most) everything! We are not sure exactly what they measure, but what we can confidently assert is that they measure the intellectual capacities of man with unquestionable exactitude! Say what you will, they are the most reliable metric of intelligence we have! It has been proven over and over that IQ tests measure the intellectual competences of individuals and nations alike!* And, having considered such arguments, I can perhaps alter my position – no, not all IQ tests are bull; so much quackery is more indicative of a duck. Perhaps the apologist of brainpower will try to refute my position with an ad hominem, one which employment I have witnessed time and again, namely the argument that I only doubt the validity of such tests because of my own low score. I do not think such an argument works against me as much as it paints the apologist in his true colors. I have nothing to prove; I have no interest in measuring di- high scores. While an IQ score would leave me indifferent one way or another, it is the apologist who has a vested interest in defending it – after all, it is his genius that relies on the number.

An impressive many standard deviations are hardly necessary to see just how poorly construed the myth of such a thing as IQ really is. For one, success is hardly a reliable concept against which to measure anything. Trying to equate it with income is hardly an intelligent solution. Van Gogh was a successful painter – significantly more successful than, say, Thomas Kinkade. Indeed, that he was not rich attests for him being an unsuccessful businessman, but his success as an artist has nothing to do with his finances – nor did his finances, I stress, have had anything to do with his talent. In this respect, interest in money is seldom a trait associated with intellectuals. At best, going by income or employment, IQ tests show only a correlation between scoring well on the test and landing a specific kind of job – a job with no exclusive claim on smart people, mind you, and certainly not a job disagreeable only to not-so-smart people. And this is if we completely ignore the socioeconomic factors regarding employment. I will not accept the argument for intellectual output for the same reasons. The idea of putting a number on intelligence is absurd, even if statistics do hint on a potentially measurable metric.

But it is not necessarily the case that even statistics are on the side of the apologist. According to Nassim Nicolas Taleb, the statistical record is not in favor of IQ tests. In "IQ is Largely a Pseudoscientific Swindle" he argues that the data tends toward a "fat tail," which results from there being too much data on one end of the graph and very little on the other (the high end) for the latter to be considered statistically relevant.[33] This lack of symmetry between low and high IQ scores (or the relatedness of each to what has been deemed *success*), casts doubt on the predictability of the hypothesis, as a mere correlation is insufficient when the standard for prediction is consistency. I ought to note here that the reader should consider looking at the graphs in the article firsthand, as my brief summary is not a thorough representation of Mr. Taleb's argument. But to present it as an analogy, to the extent that I have understood it, imagine a test designed to determine the relation between an interval of alcohol consumption and driving performance. Ten men are tested immediately after drinking. Ten others are tested a few hours after drinking. An additional ten are tested a full day after having had a drink. The result will, expectedly, show that the sooner a man attempts to drive after ingesting alcohol, the more his driving skills suffer. This does not, however, mean that a person who has not ingested any alcohol within the week drives considerably better than a man who has not ingested alcohol within the day; or that a man who has been teetotaling for decades will be the best driver among them. The correlation between alcohol consumption and driving is only relevant as long as the driver has alcohol in his blood. Likewise, Mr. Taleb argues, "'IQ' is a stale test meant to measure mental capacity but in fact mostly measures extreme unintelligence (learning difficulties)... It is via negativa not via positiva," in that it does show a correlation with poor performance, but higher values do not account for much.

I really do encourage the reader to look at the original article. It has other arguments in addition to statistics, such as the inability of IQ testing to account for "convexity of mistakes (by an argument similar to bias-variance you need to make a lot of small

---

[33] Attempts to add data to the high end only introduce noise (data too random to be considered relevant), regarding which Mr. Taleb argues "Psychologists responding to this piece do not realize that statistics is about not interpreting noise."

inconsequential mistakes in order to avoid a large consequential one,"[34] or its total deafness to the factor of personal investment in the puzzles, since "it takes a certain type of person to waste intelligent concentration on classroom/academic problems. These are lifeless bureaucrats who can muster sterile motivation." Do not mistake this for an empty insult. It relates to the concept of *skin in the game*, which, apart from its intuitive meaning, Taleb regards as the "central pillar for the organic functioning of systems," by which absence the accumulation of error without consequence causes a buildup of "asymmetric risks and misfitness" ("What do I Mean...") – removed from reality and its consequences, the kinds of positions that benefit from people with high IQ scores are likely to cause damage, not progress. In a similar tone, he lambasts IQ for being, among other things, "designed by unsophisticated nerds... poorly thought out mathematically" and "stripped of 2_{nd} order effects." These are all important points.[35] For a test evaluating one's ability to learn, IQ scoring says nothing on the subject of learning. Consider: if a man cannot solve a particular IQ puzzle, but has the solution explained to him, there is a good chance that he will thenceforth understand how to solve it and others like it. He will have learned from the experience. But IQ testing does not take this into account. An IQ test would brand him stupid on account of his initial failure. It would deny him a job, it would assault his confidence, it would have him believe that he must be ever inferior to those who got it right the first time. All because he made a small mistake, and second chances are not for smart people.

---

[34] This has to do with Taleb's argument that "Gains in technology and empirical science" rely on an "asymmetry between the gains (as they need to be large) and the errors (small or harmless)" for "luck and trial and error" to produce results ("Understanding..."). IQ tests are the opposite: there is nothing to gain, but mistakes are punished severely.
[35] Yes, including the nerd-overreach.

Some readers might be under the impression that I am a devoted follower of Mr. Taleb's, but I am not. In many instances, from politics to religion to cuisine (funnily enough, partly related to how we understand religion) we hold opposing views. But IQ testing is one thing on which we seem to blabber on the same wavelength. Especially as he comments that it is "at the bottom an immoral measure that, while not working, can put people (and, worse, groups) in boxes for the rest of their lives."

<u>What Intelligence Never Was</u>

My recent interest in the subject was initiated by a relatively historic event. It had to do with a certain American terrorist whose name I will not mention here, for I refuse to validate the fame of such an evil, perverse creature, but who should nevertheless be familiar to the reader, because the whims of fame really do favor such evil, perverse creatures. He was a man who, to summarize his cause, was so afraid of industrialization, that he went about addressing the issue by planting pipe bombs in the mailboxes of (at least in this regard) innocent people.[36] It was regarding him, that, at the time of his admittance into purgatory, I saw multiple articles online that made note of his stellar intelligence, which, counting over 160 intelligence-units, ranked him on the same level as Einstein. I thought it a peculiar point to make. If a man who revolutionized physics and was adamantly against bombing people could be, according to this system, intellectually identical to a man who revolutionized nothing and was all in favor of bombing people, whatever else this system may pretend to be, its primary epithet is (and must at all points remain) a salient complement denoting *wrong*.

A common rebuttal I hear is that intelligence is not the same as morality. To this, I must ask – why? Why should we accept the arbitrary stipulation that inferences made by intelligence are

---

[36] And they call *me* a technophobe for disliking AI.

inherently and categorically different from moral inferences –
moreover, that this former intelligence is ever *the more real*
compared to moral intelligence? I know of the attempt to avoid
answering by an appeal to moral relativism: *real intelligence cannot
be said to occupy the same semantic space as moral intelligence, because
what the IQ test measures (real intelligence) is an intelligence for
making objectively valid logical inferences, whereas moral inferences
differ between cultures, and are therefore neither objectively valid nor
logical!* I accuse such statements of hypocrisy. Conceptualizations
of logic and reality also differ between cultures – like ethics, they
also differ from one person to another. This does not mean that
the laws of logic are subjective; it only means that cultural
variation is a poor argument against the objective validity of
anything. It is only by an *a priori* negation of ethics that the
concept of moral intelligence can be removed from the category of
intelligence. This is a leap of faith. I will not accept a doctrinal
presumption as science.

I suppose another argument to address here would be the attempt
to differentiate between intelligence as a capability and intelligence
in practice, namely how one performs at an ability as opposed to
how one chooses to employ his ability – analogous, for example, to
an assassin being a good shot but a bad human being. It is by far
the best attempt to tell apart the intelligence needed for making
intelligent inferences from the processes in charge of moral
inferences. Which is how I know that there is no good argument to
set the two apart. Because, simply put, if what we test in
intelligence is an individual's ability to make the right inference,
then *every* inference is performance. The allegedly intelligent man
who is morally incompetent is not akin to the morally incompetent
sharpshooter. The latter is wholly competent at handling his
weapon; the problem is that he uses this competence for evil. The
former, however, cannot be considered competent at making
inference but prone to abusing this skill – if you try, you will have
committed yourself to the implication that behind the decision to
misuse one's intelligence, there was not in fact a wrong inference.

The man who has built his own drone and used it to attack people didn't get everything right and then misused all the things he got right – he merely got the engineering right and got everything else wrong. To go back to the sharpshooter analogy, the morally incompetent intelligent man is not a morally incompetent expert marksman, but a totally incompetent marksman. He is not the marksman who always hits his target and happens to have trained his sights on an innocent person; he is the marksman who has no concept of a target whatsoever. Sure, he may have steady hands, he may be able to adjust for humidity and wind speed, and he can even take the Coriolis Effect into account – he may even get this reference – and still, he is thoroughly ineffective, because he never knows where to aim. In short, he is stupid.

The last line of defense is to say that the terrorist with the high IQ score is after all a very intelligent man, he just happens to have made a stupid mistake. Now, I do not think that our subject is by necessity an idiot, then again, what we have is evidence of him doing something idiotic, and numbers promising that he might, hypothetically, do something smart someday. So I would not call the terrorist with the high IQ score an intelligent man who got so many things right but got one thing wrong. Rather, he got a number of insignificant things right and dumbed out where he should have thought the most. He is not a brilliant man with a flaw. He is a dimwit who can see patterns.

The most bizarre thing about this story, however, is that our Einstein-leveled terrorist cannot be really likened to the pacifist physicist even by their IQ scores, for the fact that Einstein never actually took an IQ test. That's right, the mascot of genius is only related to the poster-child of intelligence by fabrication. While there have been attempts to gauge Einstein's score had he taken such a test, by calculating such factors as his education and his academic success and (possibly) his ethnicity to see how they all match up to the scores of similarly gifted people, their circularity is too low-hanging a fruit to caress – except for the people already in the circle (but this is a classy essay). The thing with the IQ statistic is that it really does not have any persons of genius with which to boast. Humanity's greatest minds hail from before the imposition of counted intelligence. Though there are people, in the modern day, who are financially (and on occasion academically) successful and happen to have high IQ scores, their success is no more proof of intelligence than it is of being born in the right place at the right time. The same goes for them having received the training to score well (on an IQ test if nothing else).

At this point, it is more of a status symbol than anything else. Why else would one's IQ score be such a prominent subject, not among scholars, but among celebrities – people whose careers depend on their public image, people who always have something to prove, and people who have little else to show for their intelligence? It is all the more apparent that the alleged correlation between intelligence and success is a scam when you consider that a good deal of successful high-IQ-scorers are athletes, actors, and pop-singers. Are these supposed to be the proof of predicted intellectual output?

The humble-bragging is a major giveaway. When a man obsessed with IQ says that he cannot remember what his score was, but *somewhere in the 150s, something in that range, yeah,* in a disinterested almost dismissive tone, and then goes on to modestly assert, *it might be a little lower now, as I get older,* with the implication that slightly shy of super genius is still genius and in either case probably superior to yours, you can tell that IQ scores have nothing to do with measuring intelligence, but are instead a metric for measuring di– well, they do measure something, I will consent there; doubly so when the bragging is not even humble.

To be sure, it is possible, in theory, for there to be a successful man, rich and famous, a proponent of IQ testing with a very high IQ score of his own, and with mental acuity so piercing it has produced revolutionary Biblical analyses, that could, just by being all that he is, attest for IQ scores as an accurate measure of intelligence. Then again, there could also be, just as theoretically, a man of identical success, fame, ambition and profession (and, of course, an IQ score to match), I repeat, hypothetically, whose Biblical analyses are notoriously poor interpretations, and whose arrogance led him to an error that almost cost him his life, though a situation from which he emerged only more arrogant than ever. Such a man (or woman), though he (or she) might profess IQ as the standard of intelligence, is himself proof to the contrary. Of course, this is only theoretical. But imagine if (yes, hypothetically), the record-holder for high IQ was (by his own admittance) a eugenicist – moreover, one convinced that he should be the one in charge of the selective breeding he proposes. I hope you do not conclude that, given his score, we ought to give eugenics the benefit of the doubt before you have observed that his intellectual performance has demonstrably invalidated the IQ-hypothesis for good. Now that I see it in practice, the system appears to be the genetic fallacy squared: I am in the right because I am very intelligent, and I am very intelligent because the standardized testing kit told me so.

Historically, this has not been the way people have looked upon the concept – the subject of intellect; the qualifier of genius. The word *genius* originally denoted a supernatural entity, "presiding over birth, esp of a potential great or talented or otherwise remarkable person," (Partridge 1256) and intelligence comes from *intellegere* which meant "to choose from among" and so "to understand, to know, to perceive," (1750). The latter resonates with light as its metaphor, such as enlightenment meaning education, intelligent persons being described as bright, or understanding being rendered as seeing; conversely, stupidity finds its pairs in darkness. Related to perception, perhaps intelligence had something to do with conceptualization, that essential part of language that might, in the coding of its absence (indirectly, likely coincidentally, and rather rudely), explain why the synonym of mute (again, unfairly) came to mean stupid in modern speech (893). Though, I would not go there. I am not for intellectual elitism, regardless the field of study.

Either way, the etymological origins of neither genius nor intelligence suggest a quality that could work as a number. Genius was another word for talent, with an emphasis on the mystical circumstances surrounding its appearance in individuals; intelligence was the ability to know, to discover, or to learn – not something which possession alone destined a person to innate superiority. The modern conception of IQ is a significant deviation from this original understanding. Being the modern substitute for intelligence, it is presented as a means to raise somebody's intellectual reputation, and so not by knowing, but irrespective of how much he knows; when the score is high enough, he is deemed a genius – not by being talented, but in spite of his talent or lack thereof. And no, by the way, scoring high on an IQ test is not a talent on its own, comparable to singing difficult notes or painting a portrait; it is skill in a game, comparable to crosswords or Sudoku.

Admittedly, many words we use today have deviated from their original applications. My argument is not that the evolution of word meaning is necessarily wrong; it is only that what we mean by intelligence now is not rooted in a continuity refined by wisdom – it is a novel, discontinuous form, and not at all what people meant when those words were young. Nor is our modern conception of it anything like what they thought in the centuries in-between. John Stuart Mill mentions in his autobiography that, intellectually, he had an "advantage of a quarter century" ("Autobiography") over his peers by the time he was 14. But he did not attribute this to the Mill superior bloodline – the IQ gene! Rather, both he and his father credited this advantage to his education (Ford, 1049). When Mill himself uses the word genius, he does not employ it to boast of a score he got, or in reference to an innate superiority. He uses it in the context of talent ("What is Poetry?"), which is closer to its original conception. T.S. Eliot speaks of an ability to derive essential knowledge from given material, which is implicitly intelligence, seeing as he uses its opposite to signify an inability to learn: "Some men absorb knowledge, the more tardy must sweat for it. Shakespeare acquired more essential history from Plutarch than most men could from the whole British museum." This is resonant with Henry James' conception of experience to the same effect:

> ...it is an immense sensibility... suspended in the chamber of consciousness and catching every air-borne particle in its tissue. It is the very atmosphere of the mind; and when the mind is imaginative--much more when it happens to be that of a man of genius--it takes to itself the faintest hints of life, it converts the very pulses of the air into revelations.

Historically, people did not depend on numbers to promise talent – they knew talent the same way they knew a good tree: by its fruit. But fruitless as we are, especially with those in power trimming the best branches, we feel we must resort to numbers as the next best thing.

Those were more eloquent times, and so there were more things to say. There was a word standing for every perceived aspect of intellectual capability. One who learned quickly was called sharp; a person who could pick up a pattern or a disruption thereby was perceptive; if he could word it just the right way, he was eloquent; if he could make a good point with it, he was witty; if he understood mechanics easily he had a knack; if he liked math, he got bullied. But he was in no case a brilliant 160 or a satisfying 120 or a plebeian hundred. Then again, those are too many words for a modern language so indulgent in non-meaning. I said it in Pythagoras' Prison: "in his negligence of complex reality, the living representative of modernity has forsaken his vocabulary in the name of his calculator" (6). And so, there is very little to say and just as little to see and nothing to do other than to react to the pushing of your buttons; you calculate, the machine thinks. There is no use for eloquence when language is down to a one and a zero.

<u>What Intelligence still Isn't</u>

I am time and again reminded of how this particular zombie has not only infected the concept of intelligence, but has come to replace it as a wordform. I am beginning to hear, with increasing frequency, people being described not as intelligent or smart, but as varying expressions in reference to their IQ scores, most commonly *high (or low) IQ people* in informal speech, including journalistic programs, and grammatically altered versions of the same expression in formal settings. Because why claim something as indefinite as words, though they have meaning, when you can instead say things as definite as numbers, though they mean nothing? And it seems as though some process akin to inflation has taken over the connotative property of the scores, as being average is no longer *good enough*, but shameful, stupid, and not to be trusted – you do *not* want to be a university professor who scored a meager hundred; standard deviations are only a consolation prize unless they're in the genius-range (which is also the membership range, if you know what I mean), and genius is not genius unless it is a few points above that minimal genius – that cliché genius of actors and athletes – real smart people now begin to count as of 150 and above.

As I argued that a lack of performative evidence has been a motivator for the retreat to numbers, there develops, as a result, the bizarro-case where a person's intellectual performance is at risk of denigration if they are revealed to have scored unfavorably on the metric. It is an almost shameful thing to have to rely on one's intellectual work to stand for one's intellectual faculties instead of the number that, originally envisioned as a predictor of intellectual work, has come to be regarded as the determiner of intellectual work. An intellectually fulfilled person with a low IQ score is said to be *merely* determined or hard-working or disciplined – not truly intelligent like those people whose success is not due to determination, hard work, or discipline, but a miraculous birth. This is considered science.

IQ scores have really evolved, conceptually, as a term denoting a superhero-esque brainpower of sort – a mysterious ability for the performance of strange things, exclusive to the exclusively gifted, and known only to those who have it. It is not just a predictor of success, but a mystical force believed to grant special powers. People with very high IQs can casually graduate college in a single semester, they can vaguely remember the day they were born, and they can tell who did it mere ten minutes into *Columbo*. They even play old adventure games without walkthroughs. All by the virtue of seeing perpendicular lines and diagonal hints and getting the high score. If only Mill were that smart, he would not have needed intensive education to learn Latin and Greek.

The modern use of the word genius retains the elusive facet of the original meaning, but without the necessity for remarkable talent – a remarkable score will suffice. We have not acquired a more scientific understanding of intelligence; we have merely naturalized it – from the supernatural spirit to the natural gene, no less magical for its tangibility. And as moral tales of heroism become reintroduced as morally grey tales of superheroism, the question of modern cultural deterioration rears its computer-generated head. If, in its conception, the IQ score hypothesis had a sway over researchers as a form of nascent predictive verificationism, at once doomed to contradiction and immortality, it could be that its recent reemergence, or rather its naturalization as it has been conceptually and colloquially integrated among the masses, particularly the young, has been, either as a result or a motivator, related to the cultural trends that arbiter our present societal development. The hypothesis has its merit. If our present conception of beauty, feminine and masculine, has been influenced by the film industry, and to the extent that it is, in varying degrees, a subversion of standards stretching back much farther than the invention of the camera, it is not implausible that the film industry has had an influence on how we perceive virtues such as intelligence and ingenuity. We seldom get to see characters working hard. We are not shown characters regarding which character we make intelligent inferences either. Rather, we see a protagonist, conventionally attractive, and we know them to be good. It is, after all, their presentation. Likewise, we see a character, envisioned as smart, not struggling with a subject, but understanding all of it all at once – be it a janitor turned physicist, a billionaire becoming an expert on thermonuclear astrophysics overnight, or a teenager discovering a new element in their bedroom for the n_{th} time. The genius of the character is all the more poignant when it puts other (average) characters to shame. And just as we can tell the protagonist by how good-looking he is, just so we can tell an intelligent character by how good he looks while being intelligent – by how easily and gracefully and elegantly he learns and invents, without effort, making intelligence itself, otherwise invisible, look good in the process.

Do not confuse this with a cause exclusively within film presentation, by the way. It could be the reverse, with movies being a reflection of the cause, not the cause itself; as Latinate migrants were to Roman colonizers, it does facilitate the process, but it relies on pre-existing settlements to move in. I saw a snippet once from a movie (possibly a rom-com) about Shakespeare. It was a part where, almost at the deadline without having written anything, Shakespeare quickly jots down a completed play – another masterpiece created at the speed of shorthand. If the movie goes on to treat Shakespeare's plays as something he wrote overnight, then I can tell that whoever wrote (or directed) that scene has a deficit in either understanding or respect for the labor necessary to compose a play – one of Shakespearean quality, no less, in blank verse and in an Elizabethan/Jacobean context: of historical study, of minding the scansion, of foul copies, working with the actors, working around censorship, protecting the text from piracy, or accommodating the Master of the Revels. The filmmaker only respects a large audience, and he knows that what a large audience wants is a good-looking Shakespeare looking good in tights, attractively holding a quill. The actual Shakespeare does not matter, and neither does his actual genius. I believe we have forgotten what genius is, but we have convinced ourselves that, if we ever saw one, it would be pleasant on the eyes.

Anybody who has done anything worthwhile in life knows that talent is only a starter; the rest is labor. You probably also know that, without the work to prove it, talent is a fantasy at best. You can talk to a professional pianist about your finger span, your perfect pitch, or your innate sense for rhythm. But he knows that, without practice, your gifts are only good to brag with; and, once you have got a song out, the proof of your talent will not be your fingers, ears, or feet, but your song. Yet, in film, how often are musicians shown straining to learn an instrument – starting off easy but finding it hard to master, making the kinds of mistakes one hears in their least flattering singles, or struggling with the creative process in an unattractive way? Not that often. If there is a struggle, it is a romantic struggle or a social struggle or a struggle with drugs. Not the kind of unflattering labor that sullies the scene. Because genius is easy. You are either born with it, or you make movies about it.

Note that this won't fly in any other setting. Suppose I made a test for literary quotient. I could do it. It tests one's literary potential, or where they rank on a scale between Shakespeare and philistine. To test for basic competence, you are given a text by a modern fiction writer. If you can understand it, you are at least average. Onward, you will be given excerpts by classic writers, beginning with easier classics like Goldwyn, and working up to a combination of Victorians and Romantics, ordered according to their respective levels of complexity. These will be your standard deviations. Candidacy for the second percentile will be determined by Shakespeare, and for the first percentile by Shakespeare without any footnotes. The idea checks out. For one, every university professor teaching Shakespeare does indeed understand Shakespeare! We have a perfect match between the standardized tests and academic performance. Good writers too, are far more likely to have a good grasp on literature than bad writers, and especially more than functionally illiterate rubes, which gives our test the power to predict literary success. What's more, though Shakespeare himself did not take the test, we know for a fact that he would have scored highly on it, for it is a test of literary genius, and he most certainly was one. And now, that we have established the validity of our system, we will add one more thing to make it complete: scoring highly on it is enough to qualify you as a literary genius. With a good score, you may be a member of elite literary societies; in the event of an isolated apocalypse, you will be offered priority rescue; you will have employment opportunities inaccessible to the average person, though you otherwise have the same qualifications; and powerful people will conspire to selectively breed you with other literary geniuses to help create a nation of writers. I do not know if you find this humorous, but you should be able to see the absurdity in judging intelligence by IQ scores.

"But you can't be a literary genius if you haven't written anything!" you protest. *The test accurately measures your general literary intelligence*, I answer. *A score in the first or the second percentile means you are on the level of Shakespeare – what you do with this potential is up to you; you do not need to write to be a brilliant writer.* "What even is 'general literary intelligence?' The test is just an interpretation of some unrelated phrases! It is closer to a riddling game than anything else!" you ignorantly remark. *And yet it is a valid measurement*, I assure you, *because all the literarily gifted people have scored highly on it, which makes it the best system for measuring literary genius we have.* "But I know great writers who didn't do well on this test at all, yet they have created amazing works of literature!" you are impudent. *Oh, what ignorance! I exclaim. That is only because they worked hard and were dedicated to their work – certainly not literary geniuses, just your average philistines with a lot of willpower.*

Despite its absurdities, the IQ-frame remains a nigh universally accepted indicator of a quality we cannot define, except to say that it most certainly is a quality, save for instances where it contradicts the quality it was said to present, when it becomes a categorically different quality. Shortening the phrase to exclude the latter end has further distracted from the fallibility of the construct, and has given salience to the mysterious half, whereby not a score liable to factors that affect scores universally but a universal constant, independent of such contingencies, the concept of the IQ score, now upgraded to just IQ, is not to the average speaker a construct to be questioned, but an authoritative entity to be accepted, on occasion praised, and by no means doubted.

To be fair, there have been attempts by some people to demystify IQ; to normalize the superpower. *It only tests general intelligence! It only tests very specific intelligence! Even though it is very important, it is not that important!* But whereas they all address some issues, they end up fudging up other variables. Definitions of general intelligence cannot evade circularity; the specific kind of intelligence that is being tested is yet to be narrowed down to just how specific; and if IQ is not *that* important, we are yet to hear a good reason why it is considered important at all.

It is a number that can and does affect the lives of individuals, the perceptions of nations, and the very concept of thought. It is a conceptual disruption that is threatening liberty itself. Which makes it all the more ironic that it is self-proclaimed advocates of freedom who support the IQ frame the most. People who would acknowledge that humans are distinct entities with distinct human qualities, and, willing to argue for a distinctly human quality superimposed on all the others, proceed to define this quality in a frame by which we are less distinctly human than machines.

<u>An Impromptu Segue</u>

There is, I will concede, some charm in the efforts expended by some people to cope with just how little that phrase denotes. I have heard that IQ only measures a kind of intelligence that is called a *problem-solving intelligence*, which is why it is an effective measure in one field, and an ineffective measure in most others.

But this leads one to ask, what other kind of intelligence is there other than problem-solving intelligence? As if there is such a thing as a *problem-causing* or a *problem-finding* intelligence.[37] And what of the problem called *lunatics planting pipe bombs in mailboxes*? Can an IQ score help solve it? Regardless, there is no need to dwell on it, as it is a mostly innocent misconception.

I have also seen the attempt to differentiate between intelligence and intellect – intellect being how deeply and morally one thinks, whereas intelligence is (again) the mystical power that allows a man to think. Unlike the first one, this is an error with serious consequences. While making a difference between intelligent and intellectual can be useful as a shorthand for denoting sets (or combinations) of attributes, it cannot be a factual difference that could divorce the one from the other. You could use the dichotomy to describe a person as sharp but lazy, or call the janitor intelligent because he has a knack; you could say of a comedian that he writes intelligent comedy, but that he is not an intellectual by profession (or demeanor). But these are really just a convenient means of description – not an argument that an intelligent person may not be intellectual, let alone that an intellectual person may not be intelligent. The so-called intelligent person who is not intellectual is really just an intellectual slob who has at some instance shown himself capable of learning something; the so-called intellectual who is not intelligent is just a pseudointellectual.

The thing with intellectualism is that it is analogous to a dog's bite or a cat's reflexes or a bird's flight. Just as animals find enjoyment in exercising those abilities that are the most

---

[37] Even troubleshooting, where one's task is to find the problem, requires problem-solving intelligence, in that it solves the problem of diagnostics (or lack thereof); an example of problem-finding intelligence in troubleshooting would sound something like: *We have a problem – we can't figure out what's wrong!* which is, I admit, what I usually hear from troubleshooters. The same goes for problem-defining intelligence, being just a predictive-descriptive kind of troubleshooting.

impressively present in their species, so is intellect enjoyable to people in whom intelligence is the most impressively present attribute. So to say that you can have one without the other is as if to say that you have adopted an agile cat that does not jump, or a mighty American bulldog that cannot chew its meat.

So it warrants asking: how come this dichotomy even exists? Why is concern with the humanities the stupid man's imitation of intelligence – *intellectualism*, which produces nothing of value – whereas real intelligence has you scoring high on a game of lines and dots in patterns – the mark of true genius! By what reasoning did we decide the former must be inferior to cold calculation? Why is cold calculation a superpower, and intellect a feeble illusion? By what mandate did we determine that it is advisable for man, the most intelligent among animals, to utilize his intelligence only to the extent seen in less intelligent animals? It is the same thing I said earlier in the essay: we have been convinced that the metric of tangible$_2$ out of intangible$_1$ should be creatures that cannot make tangible$_2$ even out of tangible$_1$ (58).

But now, we have a new arbiter of tangible$_2$. It is an entity that, wholly composed of cold calculation, is appreciated for its ability to calculate intangible$_1$ for us. We are, after all, flawed in having too many sensibilities. Fully freed from sensibilities, the arbiter can do for us what we cannot do for ourselves – indiscriminately remove us from the equation. We say it thinks because it is so similar to us. Then again, its thinking we hold superior to ours precisely because it is nothing like our thinking. Which is how we, ignorant of the irony, conclude that our attempt at thinking is just an illusion. It is a brazen subversion of reality, the way we have accepted robotic intelligence not for what it is but for what we fantasize it to be, and so in the same breath with which we condemn our own imagination. Then again, how could we not, when our conceptual organ has suffered an injury by which far simpler concepts have proven impossibly complex? And so we conclude: if we hope to survive, we had better assimilate into the new intellectual order: scared of being erroneous meat, we can be either robotic thinkers or cunning calculators – and so we look for a dependable authority to work our buttons.

And What Intelligence Might Be

We have, just as the machine we have likened to our most human quality, come to regard our species as a conjunction of prompts and reactions. The story so far goes like this: language is liable to lossy conversion. Modern dialogue, which, in a similar vein as modern culture, is really an insufficiency of the real thing, has been exposed to elements that have led to a facilitation of the deteriorating process onto words until very recently not so intensely subjected to it. One of these has been intelligence. Our lack of noticeable intellectual achievements has made it a vague category, able to refer to more or less nothing in the present context. The vacuum in misunderstanding has been replaced by a non-meaning, composed, in part, by the mystery of the vacuum, and the numerical superstition to conceal it. The acceptance of this solution has allowed for a non-thinking object to be considered a superior thinking agent, for it is both mysterious and exceptionally competent. It is mysterious because nobody understands how it works – just as importantly, most people do not understand that it does not actually work; it is exceptionally competent because we are willing to accept the illusion. We accept it, most likely, because it appeals to our craving for convenience. This has allowed for all of the flaws of human reasoning to unite into a major non-reasoning entity. In turn, language becomes even more liable to poor transposition. The so-created stretches of intellectual vacuum invite intellectual junk, and intellectual junk demotes mankind to a non-thinking machine.

I do not know exactly who it is that would have use of so many non-thinking machines, but, disregarding names, which do not interest me, there is a certain correlation of profit and product that patterns out a trail. There is something about the affair that smacks of a drone-factory. The notion of a correlation between IQ scores and compliance begins with the statistical record, and meets further evidence as one looks into it. First, we may ask ourselves why historical IQ is a subject regarding people like Einstein and Leonardo DaVinci, but not Shakespeare, Tolstoy, or Aristotle. Not Dr. Johnson and Francis Bacon. Certainly not Florence Nightingale. It is not bards, philosophers, and revolutionaries who are regarded as possessing an intelligence worth its measure; that status is entirely allocated to very specific persons with very specific interests, predominately in mathematical, mechanical, or engineering fields. It sounds almost like the lowbrow argument against college studies – that anything outside STEM is just not worth it. Abilities not related to the demands of the market are seldom (if ever) associated with intelligence. Bluntly: will you comply to business or will you stay dumb? But that is not quite the bottom of the rabbit hole.

Do note that the people I mentioned above have questioned the version of reality they were being taught: Shakespeare criticized the perversion he noticed in high society, Tolstoy got in trouble for not being as subtle, Aristotle was almost cast out of Athens; they all challenged the narrative. They were conceptual rebels. In reference to this, you may notice that IQ does the opposite: it encourages intellectual pursuit only for a predetermined trail of breadcrumbs. It tests one's ability to notice the pattern that the tester has set out for them to find. I can imagine an appeal to the increasing difficulty of the puzzles as an argument why this is not the case – *the tester does not want you to find the pattern, that's why he hides it!* But that is off the mark. The tester may not want you to find the pattern, so as to stroke his own ego, but he is obliged to allow you to find it by the nature of the test. You can tell a pattern which creator does not intend for you to discover by the fact that you cannot discover it – not without relying on guesswork. A good example is the detective story where the narrator obscures just enough to keep the reader perpetually confused. In an IQ test, by contrast, all of the hints are on display. You are *supposed* to see them. Moreover, there is only one answer you are supposed to give – an answer that cannot vary from the will of the tester. You cannot notice a pattern outside the question itself, nor can you notice a pattern different from the ones offered to you; you can neither study it nor debate it, nor is there any reason to either study or debate something as meaningless as an IQ puzzle; the only requirement for being correct is to succumb to the master's vision. You either think the same way he does, or you are stupid. That is the price of admittance. You are not required to explain the pattern, you are not required to apply this knowledge elsewhere, you are not required to infer anything from it. You are only meant to see what you are meant to see, and to stop there. This is the new standard for intelligence. It is to agree with authority and to see no reason to dissent. It is adding nothing outside the information laid out for you. It is being a gullible yes-man.

IQ does not test intelligence as much as it trains compliance. Since compliance is usually looked down upon, this trait, so essential for success, for so we are told, has been rebranded as the cypher to intelligence, and so we believe. A spineless nerd sounds bad; a genius-level intellect sounds better. I will say it again: I cannot point fingers regarding the culprit. I do not think he is at all important. It could be a businessman looking to train staff in the demands of the market. It could be a mustache-twirling conspirator looking to mold society according to his perverse vision. It could be the masses looking to assimilate the individual into a mass hierarchy. In all cases, it is somebody in need of a calculator, advertising the virtue of calculation.

Because the use of intelligence is really not about patterns. Recognizing patters does help, but even then, intelligence is about recognizing the *right* pattern. The pattern in nature, the pattern in logic, the pattern in human behavior – not the pattern somebody made up and had printed in a test. There is certainly a survival benefit in being able to recognize the color pattern of the coral snake – provided you also recognize the concept of venom and the concept of human life. But to extrapolate this so that you paint a scarlet king snake a complex pattern, and say that to be able to read it reveals a power over the secrets of the universe, is more shamanism than science. Because recognizing patterns is to intelligence as big ears are to stature. There is a correlation. And that is all there is. Intelligence can only ever be a fact when it is applied to reality. This includes abstract reality. Whenever the case is not such, all the parts one mistakes for the whole (pattern-recognition, short-term memory, calculation) are at best perks (perchance the enablers of hobbies), and, in extreme cases, tools of lunacy. As such, intelligence and sanity must be regarded as one, like a guitar and strings, or life and heartbeat.

Intelligence is the facet of sanity covering the part of the world that is reasonably tangible. Everything that aids sanity in this regard, be it logic or calculation or recognizing patterns is a handmaiden of rationality. Every expression denoting a mental affinity, like witty or sharp or perceptive, is a talent of this general ability – a giftedness in one aspect, distinct from the others, but equal to them in purpose. Now, an orchestra needs many talents (diverse talents), to make the best music, and so, the discussion on specialization versus diversification is always a good one to have. A lone wolf in my early adolescence, I have, for the most part, triumphed as a Jack of all trades, except for those times I have proven myself a Jack of all asses. In time, I have grown fond of teamwork. But, I digress. Though I have implicitly criticized bookworms elsewhere, I will take their side in this argument. Even relying entirely on book-knowledge is its own kind of intelligence – it is not rote recital or an inability for independent thought; on the contrary, it is an homage to the world's intellectual legacy; a talent for expressing this to the fullest. As such, it should neither be entrusted everything in isolation, nor should it be derided in isolation. The musical connoisseur is just as respected as the orchestra, though he does not play in it.

Now, I do not argue against the possibility of genetic factors arbitrating intelligence, or the degree to which a person has it.

Personally, I have no doubt that it is a mental faculty, and it is obviously related to something in the brain. It is why I am not a proponent of the multiple intelligences hypothesis. While it does remedy some issues of the IQ swindle, a hypothesis that says that the engineer and the schoolteacher can be equally intelligent, only in different ways, really loses this reasonable merit when it says that they are also intellectual equals to the talented dancer. Anyone who has spent time around professional athletes can reject the multiple intelligences hypothesis on empirical grounds. Intelligence must be of the intellect. But intellect cannot be unless it is of sanity, or the will seeking reality. Even an ignorant man may be taught, and even a slow man can eventually understand a complex matter, provided he is willing to learn. It is only an insane person (the degree of insanity varies) that is impossible to teach. When you hear a man saying extremely stupid things, you can usually trace this problem to an issue of character: to overconfidence, or boldness, or self-affirmation, be it self-aggrandizement or self-deprecation; to laziness or rashness or naivety. Mental blocks that may or may not correlate with an IQ test are factored in only later. Because man did not step out of the caves to look for patterns in the fire – I do not buy the trippy LSD origin theory. Rather, man became civilized as he saw himself for a man, he saw the world for the world, and he saw that it was good to know it.

Why Sanity Must Be

If intelligence and sanity are one, and if the intelligent are those gifted, according to this argument, to learn and to make inferences, then the importance of sanity is a given. Moreover, seeing as sanity is a movement of the will, then sanity is a prerequisite of freedom, as only the liberated will can pursue truth, i.e. only a free person is free to be sane. An idiot, no matter the kind, will always be a slave to his idiocy, as will an insane person toil for his lunacy. Any group of disassociated, uneducated, or confused people are a coerced set of people; if sufficiently big, they make up a coerced nation – laws notwithstanding, the degree of coercion can alter but the taste of slavery, not the fact of it.

There is no liberty like understanding; like being free to reach the correct conclusion. This is the chapter where the introductory section meets the others. I began with the argument that evil begins as stupidity. Now, I have argued that stupidity is closer to insanity than what we have so far mistakenly considered the antonym of intelligence. Yes, evil is insanity. And in that truth is concealed the fullness of the argument.

One might ask, *if evil people are insane, are insane people then, logically, evil?* Not necessarily. Insane people can be evil, but they can also be merely innocently deranged. You do not need me to tell you this. Mental illness is a known phenomenon. It is an obstruction to sanity. The institution concerned with mental health, however, while it does (try to) address mental illness, provided removing the obstruction is at all possible, and hence, it does (claim to) treat insanity, does not seem to have much of an effect on promoting sanity. You may consider this the second controversial chapter. Sanity must be because mental health has failed.

I mean that conceptually *and* effectively, with the latter being an effect of the former. If the emergent culture is anything to go by, we see a decrease in sanity and mass reliance on chemicals to make up for its burden; madmen exulting and sane people going mad; less people thinking they can make sense of things and more therapists advocating against the making of sense. Given the context, character quirks that might lead the average person to a therapist are a symptom not of derangement but of sanity going on red alert; ironically, those who do not require help as they thrive in a maddening world are those who (ought to be) in the direst need of help – the damning damned who do not give a damn. The absurdity becomes a tragedy, however, when this evolves into therapists *curing* sane people by teaching them to resemble the loon so as to free themselves from the nervous agitation: my once passionate, idealistic friends becoming hedonistic slobs; disinterested in what is right, thoroughly tolerant of the wrong around them (including the wrong inflicted on them), and completely assimilated into a culture of placid pleasures – not finally free from the reins of their depression, but having found that the reins are not so bad if they consent to also wear blinders.

Regarding the relatedness of mental health to an accurate picture of the world, ideationally and practically, it feels as if nobody has any idea of anything, but somebody must be paid to pretend that he does. Reality seldom being quite as bleak as it appears, however, I do not think the issue is quite as dire. There are good therapists in the world. Psychology has accomplished much. I do not wish to see anyone (even bad psychologists) lose their jobs. Nobody is beyond redemption. I only suggest that they reconsider their priorities. I said it earlier in this chapter, and I've been saying it throughout my entire essay: the issue is in the mishandling of concept. It is there that the modern psychologist ought to look for the reason mental health has gone to hell. Scientifically, we have gained a better understanding of human behavior. For this, I salute psychologists throughout history. But alongside that (or in spite of it), we have developed complete confusion regarding the human mind. And this is what modern psychologists must address.

I was surprised to learn that students of psychology (graduates and master's students included) could not care less for philosophy of the mind. Before conversing with these people, I assumed the mind would be their major interest – not statistics on how animals help students get better grades. No offense, by the way. Because it is hardly reasonable that a profession that is, in its essence, a practicing philosophy, should be practiced by people disinterested in philosophy. That just invites conceptual corruption, which, from what I have gathered from conversation, has had its impact already. It is not much of an achievement to define mental health as a mental state that allows a person to be productive, and then trivialize his problems as long as they do not impede on his daily workload. In this sense, mental health is just a watered down version of stoicism with a sprinkling of dopamine, which is really just another water seller in the rain – with somewhat spiked drinks. It is not conceptual progress either to enrich the definition with the assumption that a person, if mentally healthy, will be in the position to develop himself to his fullest potential, then limit this vague expectation with the caveat that the aforementioned potential must be within reasonable expectations: *it is not reasonable of you to expect such success, it is narcissistic personality disorder – a protagonist complex, even!* As if a man is not the protagonist in his own life. It allows the therapist to diagnose a dreaming man with one complex (an offshoot of ambition), and label him with another the moment he wakes up (an offshoot of dejection). Not to mention, it has scary implications in regards to political governing. One way to ensure that nobody can aspire to crazy ambitions, such as to be a master pianist, is to ensure that nobody can afford to own a piano – ought we then to throttle the economy in the name of mental health? Nor is it good conceptualization to have happiness as an integral part of your definition; especially not when you have defined happiness as a state of contentedness wholly independent of one's problems – something from within, something that can be solved with a different attitude, problems notwithstanding, a smile, problems still standing, soma, problems accumulating. In such conceptual frivolity, a therapist would see nothing wrong in a philosophical zombie or a functional artificial intelligence unit (though these could work in science fiction), because, to him, they would be the epitome of mental health as long as they perform well at work; as long as they have the semblance of friends, and as long as they do not complain. Then again, a righteous man seeing injustice getting angry at this injustice is considered a red flag – not because of the injustice, mind you, but because he has become too angry to remember he ought to smile.

Let us contrast mental health to sanity. The concept of sanity is clear. It stands for an accurate understanding of reality – what is in your head and what is in the world should be compatible with one another. The concept of mental health, however, being a (vaguely) medical term, cannot afford that kind of humanism in its definition: an appeal to reason, an appeal to subjective experience, and an appeal to virtue are arguments lacking in verifiable principles. Mental health must be above them. And so, mental health has tried to ignore them. On the one hand, a person's beliefs are considered irrelevant because we cannot rely on reason as the standard by which to confirm or rule out insanity – *that*, many argue, would be essentialism, which is forbidden. A person's behavior, by contrast, though considered a practical measure of mental health, cannot describe him as honorable, just, or inhuman, but only as obsessive, conflictive, or stable (respectively). This is why a cunning sociopath can evade a therapist, but a sane person with a quick temper cannot be allowed to hold on to his personality. Since virtue, proclaimed a subjective thing, is not to be considered in the mental health equation, performance can only ever be a balance between aligning with societal expectations and ideological leniencies, by which the professional proclamation of health is, conceptually, more of an approval than fact.

It is precisely in what it lacks that the concept of mental health conflicts with a fundamental fact of the human psyche – as fundamental as those employment qualifications that are never mentioned, for they are supposed to be understood: we cannot have a sane individual who is not a moral individual. A moral individual is by necessity reasonable, and therefore intelligent. But an intelligent, moral person cannot thrive in an unjust world – not very jovially. To try to therefore inhibit his qualities so as to optimize societal functionality, this functionality being an arbitrary contract between authoritarian licenses and plebeian preferences, is to eliminate individuality altogether and instead promote a homogenous mass of stupidity, which, I have already argued, is tantamount to insanity. In philosophy, and in practice, there is something wrong with the conception of mental health.

Again, I do not consider psychology a bogus practice; psychology has made great contributions to a unique body of knowledge for which mankind cannot show but the profoundest gratitude. My argument is simply that the idea of mental health seems to be lacking in some crucial aspects, and its adherents had better address them if they are to make the concept work.

It is for this reason that I choose sanity. Mental health claims to remove obstructions to sanity. I have no doubt that it does. Where it fails is that it does not care to add sanity in the process. Unfortunately, that is what insanity really is: the privation of the positive. Insanity is a deficit of the sensibility by which one can conceive a consistent, reliable understanding of reality. It is being wrong and being fine with it. It is being stupid and being proud, which inevitably leads to evil, as idiocy and lunacy, tightly related from the start, become indistinguishable. Ergo, sanity must be. We have no substitute for it.

To go back to the question of a mentally sound person doing evil, what we really see are people who, not having obstacles to their sanity such as a physical injury or chemical imbalances, they yet lack the substance on which the human mind functions: the will directed towards reality. Why this should be the case, I can speculate and I can poeticize – but the simplest way to put it is that they do not know any better. They ride with the Raider and the Aristocrat and the Madman, they pillage and they conquer, they consult strange machines, they worship in cults, and it is all for nothing – for an immortality, perhaps, that they seek in all the wrong places. They have been infected by the virus of non-meaning, bitten by the zombie-words that roam the cities, turning into the philosophical zombies of prompt and reaction, and all for that initial misunderstanding of a concept that, I warned you, I can merely speculate. Perhaps it is the concept of liberty. Perhaps. But one thing is certain: of our brothers, they are the least brotherly. They are ever the enslavers, though they are also the most heavily enchained; and brotherly though we must be to them, in this dark new world, winged things can only flap in darkness: some as nightingales, some as bats, and some as demons – and idealism aside, unable to see clearly, it is only by a devotion to sanity that we can tell which is which.

Another World

In this world, it is so. In another, daylight might bring clarity. I began this essay with the assertion that mere intellectual rambling, regardless the genre, is not much of a literary achievement. I have also argued that problem-solving intelligence is the only kind of intelligence that exists if the concept must include the word problem. So I ought to propose something to remedy the fall I have described – or to at least make the reader feel better about it. And I will propose something, I believe, that is of more essence than just a feel-good conclusion: the generic promise of hope to leave on a high note, or alternatively a stoic affirmation to make the gloomy note manly – these are really not my style. I would rather be profound about it – whether you like it or not.

In my previous essay, I asked *what is a man* (in a different context), and I added a footnote that the cocksure reader should not default to the *adult human male* answer and fail to anticipate the response. The response is, if you can by now guess the way I think: *what is an adult?* and you may watch the cocksure reader fumble for an answer, "it's a... uh... adult is when you turn eighteen!" *Pythagoras' Prison* was about the replacement of meaning with numbers, and such an answer would prove my argument, irrespective of the gender controversy. To be sure, the question of man in regards to gender, short of XY18, is a nuanced issue, and, ultimately, unless adulthood is a black-and-white fact independent of society, the concept of man, beyond a penis-support mechanism, is indeed a social construct. Which is not to say that just because one side of the debate is proud to be stupid, the other is not just as stupidly proud. The cartographer (79) does not stop there. That gender is a construct does not conclude the discussion. But I think it has been taken in the wrong direction altogether. Because it should not be a question of definition, but a question of origin, namely the origin of the disagreement. The key, I believe, might be historical; arguably sociological. Biology really does not factor in just yet.

Because this was not a common discussion in medieval society – among the peasant stock or the traders the merchants the soldiery or even the nomads. And something that those people had, as if to compensate for all that they lacked (that we now happen to need the most, as if a tax for all we can afford to throw away), was a common experience of life: common goals; common sights; a common tongue. They all shared a facet of reality, and they all agreed on it. No, they did not live as if in paradise; there certainly were disputes and conflict and not very fun common experiences, even among the common folk with the common lives and the common tongue. And yet, their core conceptual matrix remained a common conceptual matrix. Their frame of reference, the experience that shapes the category, was one and the same.

So when one looks at the gender discussion in the modern day, the real question should not be *what is a man or a woman*, but *at what point did we become so discordant with one another* that even such basic concepts as man and woman, that have survived millennia with the same intension and the same extension, have now turned into a conceptual battlefield for the masses? And the answer might be in the fact that there is no longer a shared experience of life. The alienating trend has affected humanity so deeply that we now speak languages foreign to one another despite their form, and foreign even to the linguistic tradition from which they have emerged. We are not dealing with a problem of gender identity or heteronormativity or degeneracy or a war on Christianity – no, we are dealing with extreme loneliness. We are dealing with insanity (on both sides) by isolation, and cultism (on both sides) by this same isolation. It is about many people, scattered in about as many experiences, thrown about in as many ambitions, and divided by as many times the disagreements – disagreements with oneself not least: confused as we are, assuming in our intimate confusions that the confusion of others must be greater than ours. One side, scared to fight slavery, has succumbed to pretending that slavery is just fine. Unable to oppose the villain, they have channeled their rage at people unhappy to be his henchmen. The other side, just as scared by their enslaver, have opted to pretend that he is their friend. Unable to stand on their own, they have decided that the villain should stand for them. In the meantime, people grow lonelier, language gets weirder, and reality becomes thinner.

In ignoring the real problem, we have lost touch with the one true answer regarding the gender-question: what is a man? Then again, have I not foreshadowed it at the beginning of the essay? We know the answer already: what is a man? A man is your brother. From there, you might ask, *And what is a manly man?* A manly man is a man who treats others brotherly. When at least two sides can agree with that, we can have an honest discussion – whichever the outcome, the disagreement itself will be barely a nuisance, if even that. As soon as we have established common ground, as soon as both sides come to look unfavorably upon the enemy instead of each other (whoever he may be), and redirect the ambition for narrative to labor towards truth, the truth of brotherhood above all, the elusive enemy will at last begin to show himself: it will be whoever wishes to revert back to questions not of inquiry but of confusion, who would discourage contemplation on all but the intellectually cheapest subjects, who would reform education in but two courses: a module for calculators and a module for idiots. He would establish a philosophy by which both are preferable to language, which he despises, and maintain a worldview impervious to either truth or sanity, which he considers equally as irrelevant.

On the bright side, it is for this same reason, the declouding of intention, that friends will become as visible as stars in the night sky. Of course we would. If knowledge is illumination, and brotherhood is equality in kind, and knowledge means intelligence and intelligence means sanity and sanity means virtue and virtue is brotherhood, by which brotherhood is the light of the world, then, anything other than these correlates with the darkness all around. The contrast will make it easier to tell friend from void. Just keep in mind: the North Star is the cartographer.

I told you I would make it profound. And I warned you that you may not like it. I *always* deliver. But at least it will have inspired a new thought – an *outside the box* kind of thing, even though it may have never escaped Pandora's Box (though it was a jar) for all the good it has accomplished. In my next essay, I will talk about (as of recorded history) the most effective means of opposing confusion – I will talk about art; I will define it and analyze some of it, in my own way. I will then talk about some other things I see related to it (again, in my own way), which you will have to see for yourselves.

Until then, I wish you, Dear Reader, a good time as you go about life, and a conceptually wonderful adventure in thinking the things most deserving of your thoughts.

In good faith,
Hank Youngman.

END of PART II

References and such – for those who really *really* care...

"Abstract Art." *Encyclopedia Britannica.*
  https://www.britannica.com/art/abstract-art

Bowdle, Brian and Dedre Gentner. "Metaphor as Structure
  Mapping." *The Cambridge Handbook of Metaphor and Thought,*
  edited by Raymond M. Gibbs, Jr., Cambridge University Press,
  2008.

"Corpus of Contemporary American English." *English-
  Corpora.org.*

"Corpus of Historical American English." *English-Corpora.org.*

"iWeb: the 14 Billion Word Web Corpus." *English-Corpora.org.*

Deep Purple. "Fortuneteller." *Slaves and Masters,* 1990. Written by
  Jon Lord, Ian Anderson Paice, Roger David Glover, Richard
  Blackmore, and Joe Lynn Turner.

Denis, Maurice. "Definition of Neo-Traditionalism." 1890.

Eliot, Thomas Stearns. "Tradition and the Individual Talent."
  The Egoist, 1919.

Ford, George H., editor. "John Stuart Mill." *The Norton Anthology
  of English Language,* vol. 2, 4th ed., edited by M.H. Abrams.
  W.W. Norton & Company, Inc., 1979.

Franklin, Benjamin. "From Benjamin Franklin to Sarah Bache, 26
  January, 1784." *Founders Online,*
  https://founders.archives.gov/documents/Franklin/01-41-02-
  0327#BNFN-01-41-02-0327-fn-0015 Original source: *The Papers of
  Benjamin Franklin, vol. 41, September 16, 1783, through February 29,
  1784.* edited by Ellen R. Cohn, Yale University Press, 2014.

Glucksberg, Sam. "How Metaphors Create Categories – Quickly." *The Cambridge Handbook of Metaphor and Thought*, edited by Raymond W. Gibbs, Jr., Cambridge University Press, 2008.

Goethe, Johann Wolfgang. *The Sorrows of Young Werther*. 1774. Translated by R.D. Boylan, edited by Nathen Haskell Dole, Project Gutenberg, 2009.

Hanks, Patrick Wyndham. "Metaphoricity is Gradable," *Corpus-based Approaches to Metaphor and Metonymy*, edited by Anatol Stefanowitsch and Stefan Th. Gries. Mouton de Gruyter, 2006.

James, Henry. "The Art of Fiction." *Longman's Magazine*, September 1884. https://public.wsu.edu/~campbelld/amlit/artfiction.html

Joyce, James. *Finnegan's Wake*. 1939.

Kierkegaard, Søren. "Preface," *The Sickness unto Death*. 1849. Princeton University Press, 1941.

Koontz, Dean. "A Note to the Reader," *Ticktock*. Ballantine Books, 1996.

Kövecses, Zoltan. *Metaphor, a Practical Introduction*, 2nd ed., Oxford University Press, 2010.

MacDonald, George. "It shall not be Forgiven," "The New Name," *Unspoken Sermons*. 1867. Produced by Jonathan Ingram and Charlie Kirschner, Project Gutenberg, 2005.

Mill, John Stuart. *Autobiography*, 1873. Produced by Marc D'Hooghe and David Widger, Project Gutenberg, 2003.
---. "What is Poetry?" *The Monthly Repository of Theology and Great Literature*, 1833. nsce.ac.uk/periodicals/mruc/.

Partridge, E. *Origins: A Short Etymological Dictionary of Modern English*, Routledge, 1966.

Puzo, Mario. *The Dark Arena*. Ballantine Books, 1955.

Skeat, Walter William. *Concise Etymological Dictionary of the English Language*, Perigee Books, 1980.

Steinman, James Richard. "Water Seller's Song," performed by Barry Keating, 1971.
--- . "I'd do Anything for Love (But I Won't Do That)." *Bat out of Hell II: Back into Hell*, performed by Michael Lee Aday ft. Lorraine Crosby. Ocean Way, Hollywood, 1993.

Taleb, Nassim Nicholas. "IQ is Largely a Pseudoscientific Swindle." *Medium*. 2019. medium.com/incerto/iq-is-largely-a-pseudoscientific-swindle-f131c101ba39.
---. "Understanding is a Poor Substitute for Convexity (Antifragility)." *Edge*. 2012. https://www.edge.org/conversation/nassim_nicholas_taleb-understanding-is-a-poor-substitute-for-convexity-antifragility
---. "What do I mean by Skin in the Game? My Own Version." *Medium*. 2018. https://medium.com/incerto/what-do-i-mean-by-skin-in-the-game-my-own-version-cc858dc73260

"Tangible." *Merriam-Webster.com Dictionary*.

The Bible. New International Version, 3rd ed. Biblica, 2011.

Youngman, Hank. "Chapbook #3." *The Chapbooks Trilogy*. 2022.
---. *The Playwright*. 2022.
---. *Pythagoras' Prison*. 2023.

Žižek, Slavoj. "Slavoj Žižek 'And so on.'" *YouTube*, uploaded by Odub, 5 March 2017, https://www.youtube.com/watch?v=Boc2LjKdqqw.

<u>In this Series...</u>

<u>Pythagoras' Prison</u>

In this introductory essay, the author explains the structure of our conceptual prison, the danger of its illusion, and the circumstances surrounding its creation – ideological, practical, and personal.
Through an elaborate metaphor of crime, toymakers, and an asylum, Pythagoras' Prison is written to illustrate the modern fallacy and to refocus the purpose of thought onto its original trajectory.

<u>An Essay Concerning Human Misunderstanding</u>

An *Essay Concerning Human Misunderstanding* is the central entry in the eponymous series. It is a meditation on a selection of contemporary passions that burden the modern citizen. Relying on linguistic science, philosophical appeal, and human curiosity, it locates their origin in a conceptual error, which discovery is at once to the reader's satisfaction and the means of recovery.

<u>Bards, Robots, and Hordes</u>

A treatise on defeat as an outcome not at all humiliating: sometimes, it is not triumph that determiners winner from loser. There follow three essays: on art; artificial intelligence; and mankind's regression into the primitive commune known as a horde – an uncaring, uneducated, and untrusting population. It is about deception by ornament, an unusual orphanhood, and conceptual deterioration... a conclusion just shy of optimistic goes without saying.

<u>Also by Hank Youngman...</u>

The Chapbooks Trilogy

A printed collection of 50 poems and 3 essays, divided in three parts according to form and subject matter: *Ambition in Vain*, *Songlets*, and *Chapbook #3*.
Each part can also be purchased independently as a digital copy.

It Comes with the Territory

A science-fiction mystery adventure with an emphasis on the real-world factors that enable the grounds for the plot. Written in the tradition of classic science fiction, *It Comes with the Territory* aims to entertain, in as far as the reader enjoys mystery adventures, as well as to inspire thought, in as far as the reader is accustomed to thinking.

The Playwright

Set in a plot that is in the same measure natural and supernatural, *The Playwright* is a unique take on the ghost story as narrated in a modern context – a work of mystery, suspense, and light horror, it is an ideal read for the modern enthusiast of the genre.

A Righteous Agenda

A work of mystery, suspense, and light satire that aims to provide an intriguing set of characters and events, with a twist that is subtly foretold yet remains just out of grasp until the conclusion.